Russian Steam Locomotives

H M Le Fleming & J H Price

RUSSIAN STEAM LOCOMOTIVES

DAVID & CHARLES : NEWTON ABBOT

ISBN 0 7153 5495 7

First published by John Marshbank Ltd	1960
First published by David & Charles	1968
Second, revised edition	1972

Printed in Great Britain
by Redwood Press Limited Trowbridge Wiltshire
for David & Charles (Publishers) Limited
South Devon House Newton Abbot Devon

Contents

List of Locomotive Classes

Class		Introduced	Type	Pages	Plates
A	(А)	1878	2–6–0	26	
a	(а)	1895	0–6/6–0 Mallet	28, 33	
AA20	(АА20)	1934	4–14–4	51, 52	41
Ad	(Ад)	1892	4–6–0	28	15
B	(Б)	1908	4–6–0	37	19
Ch	(Ч)	1879	0–8–0	27	4
E	(Э)	1912	0–10–0	32, 39, 40, 46	27
Eg	(Эг)	1921	0–10–0	40	
Egk	(Эгк)	1933	0–10–0 Condensing	90	65
Em	(Эм)	1931	0–10–0	47, 48, 49	28, 30
Emk	(Эмк)	1937	0–10–0 Condensing	93	
Er	(Эр)	1935	0–10–0	48, 49	29
Esu	(Эсу)	1944	0–10–0	48, 49	
Eu	(Эу)	1926	0–10–0	47, 49, 95	
Ě	(Ѣ)	Project	0–10–0 4-cyl. comp.	33	
F	(Ф)	1872	0–6/6–0 Fairlie	26	16, 17
F	(Ф)	1915	2–10–0 4-cyl.	33	
FD	(ФД)	1931	2–10–2	53, 54, 55	42, 43, 44
FD18	(ФД18)	1943	2–10–4	55	
FDk	(ФДк)	1939	2–10–2 Condensing	93	
G	(Г)	1900	4–6–0 2-cyl. comp.	30	20
Hy	(V)	1908	0–8–0	31	
Ï	(I)	1903	2–4/4–0 Mallet	29	
I	(И)	1909	2–8–0	31	
IS	(ИС)	1932	2–8–4	55, 56	45, 46
K	(К)	1908	4–6–0	30	21
Kh	(Х)	1895	2–8–0 Compound	28	
Ku	(Ку)	1911	4–6–0	30, 38	
L	(Л)	1945	2–10–0	72, 73	54, 55, 71
LK	(ЛК)	Project	2–8–4	60	
Lp	(Лп)	1915	4–6–2 4-cyl.	31, 41, 73	31
LV	(ЛВ)	1952	2–10–2	74, 75, 76	56

Class		Introduced	Type	Pages	Plates
Mr	(Мр)	1927	4–8–0 3-cyl.	45, 46	32
N	(Н)	1892	2–6–0	27, 31, 36, 37	10, 12
O	(О)	1889	0–8–0	27, 34, 35, 36	6, 7, 8, 9, 72
OR21	(ОР21)	1954	2–10–2	74	
OR23	(ОР23)	1949	2–10–4 Experimental	74, 95, 96	
P	(П)	1945	2–10–0 (see L class)		
Pb	(Пб)	1891	4–4–0 Tandem comp.	28	
Ph	(Ѳ)	1903	0–6/6–0 Mallet	29	18
Pp	(Пп)	1898	4–4–0 Tandem comp.	28	13
Pt	(Пт)	1907	4–6–2 semi-tank	29	14
P34	(П34)	1949	2–6/6–2 Articulated	74	73
P36	(П36)	1950	4–8–4	76, 77, 78	Frontispiece 57, 58, 59
P38	(П38)	1954	2–8/8–4 Articulated	78, 80	74
4P	(4П)	1935	0–4–0 T	83	
5P	(5П)	1935	0–6–0 T	83	
9P	(9П)	1936	0–6–0 T	83	61, 62
R	(Р)	1899	2–8–0 Tandem comp.	28	22
S	(С)	1901	2–6–2	31, 32, 38, 39	33
Sh,a	(ША)	1943	2–8–0	64	39
Shch	(Щ)	1905	2–8–0	30, 36	23, 24, 25
Schch,ch	(Щч)	1927	2–8–0	30, 36	
SO17	(СО17)	1935	2–10–0	56, 57	49, 50, 72
SO18	(СО18)	1945	2–10–0	57	48
SO19	(СО19)	1936	2–10–0 Condensing	57, 90, 91, 92	
Su	(Су)	1925	2–6–2	43, 44, 45, 95	34, 35, 36, 75
Sum	(Сум)	1940	2–6–2	44, 45, 93	
Sv	(Св)	1915	2–6–2	32	
Ta	(ТА)	1931	2–10–4	51	
Ta	(ТА)	1933	0–6–0 T	83	63
Tb	(Тб)	1931	2–10–2	51	
TE	(ТЭ)	1943	2–10–0 (ex-German)	67	51, 52
Tg	(Тг)	1933	0–6–0 T	83	

Class		Introduced	Type	Pages	Plates
TL	(ТЛ)	1943	2–10–0 (ex-German)	68	
TM	(ТМ)	1946	4–8–0 (Hungarian)	69, 70	
TP1	(ТП1)	1939	2–10–2 Experimental	95, 96, 109	
Tu23	(ТУ23)	1939	2–10–0 (ex-Polish)	62	53
U	(У)	1903	4–6–0 4-cyl. comp.	30	
Uu	(УУ)	1912	4–6–0 4-cyl. comp.	30	
V	(В)	1896	4–6–0 Compound	28	
V5	(В5)	1937	0–4–4 High pressure	95	
Y	(Ы)	1909	0–8–0	31	26
Ya	(Я)	1896	2–6–0	27	11
Ya	(Я)	1932	4–8–2–2–8–4 Garratt	53	40
Ye	(Е)	1916/44	2–10–0	33, 41, 42, 65, 94	37, 38
Ye,f	(ЕФ)	1894	2–10–0 Compound	28	
Signs					
Hard,n	(Ън)	1910	2–8–2 T	30	
Soft	(Ь)	1899	0–6–0 T	82	60
Soft	(Ь)	1929	2–10–2 T	42	
Types					
	2–3–2	1938	4–6–4	58, 59, 60	47
	2–4–2	1950	see P36 Class		
Numbers					
	6998	1938	4–6–4 see Class 2–3–2		
	8000	1939	2–8–2 Experimental	95, 96	
	8001	1948	2–10–2 Experimental	95, 96	
Name					
(*Drug*)		1951	4–8–2 3-cyl. comp.	76, 109	
Unclassed					
Industrial			0–4–0 T		
Forestry (N.G.)			0–8–0	87, 88	66, 67
Childrens' Pioneer (N.G.)			0–8–0	88, 89	68, 69

Introduction

Although the curtain between Russia and the West is gradually being lifted, there is still an air of secrecy about certain Soviet institutions that inevitably invites the curiosity of those connected with similar ones in the West. One such institution is the railway system, which to the U.S.S.R. has a strategic importance much greater than in other countries so that, although visitors to Russia frequently travel by train from place to place, the railways themselves are still included among the subjects that foreign tourists are not supposed to photograph. This adds a certain spice not usually found in the study of railways and the interest thus engendered added to the driving force in the researches which led to this book.

One aim of the authors has been to satisfy, by putting on paper the results of their own researches, some of the interest that undoubtedly exists among railway enthusiasts and historians regarding the Soviet Union's stock of steam locomotives, filling in those parts of the picture that have not been mentioned in the official press releases. In the main the book sets out to deal with two aspects: the types and classes of steam locomotive in use, and the quantity existing of each class.

For such a study, in the case of Russia, two different lines of approach are required: that of the engineer and that of the archaeologist. Few engineers are trained in archaeological deduction and few amateur excavators are engineers, but if the two join forces—the one to seek out information, the other to interpret and present it—something historically useful may emerge. In the field of Russian railway activities, as in many others, two heads are certainly better than one, and if parts of this book read like a mystery story while others resemble an engineering textbook, it is only a sign of one or other of the author's being happily at work in his chosen field of activity.

Much of the information in this book is historical, for although access to railway information has been greatly eased during the past three or four years, this applies only to current developments and not to the events of the recent past. The most recent Russian innovations in the railway field have been described in the Western technical press and the present-day railway engineer can study and compare new Soviet techniques with those of his own country, but the years of secrecy have left their mark with a lingering curiosity to know what the Russian railways were doing yesterday and the the day before, when little or no information filtered through. Especially is this the case among students of the steam locomotive.

It is a curious fact, although no more than a coincidence, that the relaxing of controls on Russian railway information coincided almost exactly with the end of new steam locomotive construction. Diesel and electric locomotives have been built in large numbers since 1956 and ample details of them are now available; but even larger numbers of steam locomotives were built between 1947 and 1956, yet most of them went virtually unrecorded. It is very desirable that this 'lost generation' of steam locomotives should be described and illustrated, for they form the final chapter in the long and distinguished story of the steam locomotive in the lands now comprising the Soviet Union.

With this in mind the authors, both of whom have travelled in Russia and seen Russian railway operation at first hand, have tried in this book to trace the story of the Russian steam locomotive from its inception; first, with a backward glance at the nineteenth century with the early moves towards locomotive standardisation and railway unification, up to the first World War; secondly, by describing in detail the present steam locomotive stock, which includes pre-1917 survivors and engines built during the Revolution, the first and second Five-Year Plans, the second World War and post-war years, up to the time when main-line steam locomotive production finally ceased in 1956. (References in the text to the present time should be taken as relative to January 1958, when work was begun on this book.)

12

Fulfilling our aim has not been easy owing to the extraordinary dearth, already noted, of information on the numbers of locomotives built in each class. This has often in the past caused prototype and experimental locomotives to be confused with standard types, and some former writers on Russian locomotives have, for instance, given very full details of the solitary 4–14–4 or the ten American-built freight locomotives of 1931, while ignoring altogether the many hundreds of 0.10.0 freight engines built during the same period. In this way a somewhat distorted picture of Russian railway motive power has come into being, and one of our objects has been to correct this by establishing the relative importance of each steam locomotive class in terms of the numbers built and work performed.

In the absence of detailed official statistics the method we have used is to identify and describe the various numbering systems used for Russian steam locomotives, which we believe has not been done before. We have then tabulated the running numbers of all the locomotives seen, reported or photographed, using this data to determine the approximate total for each class. It will be realized that in dealing with Russian locomotives the oft-despised 'loco-spotter' has a definite contribution to make to the sum total of our knowledge, and this study has only been made possible by the willing co-operation of many friends in Britain, France, Germany, Austria, Switzerland and the U.S.A., who have added their own valuable observations to the data that we ourselves have collected. Some of the observations go back to the early nineteen-twenties, while others were contributed by students of the loco-motive who served in Russia with the German armies in 1941–5, or were in that country later as prisoners of war. Many of our helpers, perhaps understandably, prefer to remain anonymous, but to all of them we express our most grateful thanks for their valuable assistance, freely given. Without them the assessing of locomotive class totals by this method would not have been practicable.

Another field in which we have depended largely on the work of others is that of illustrations, for although the authors between them have photographed on their travels about a dozen of the locomotive classes described, their efforts have been surpassed both in quality and quantity by pictures taken by others and made available to them. Throughout the book we have given precedence to photographs taken in Russia showing locomotives actually in traffic, and to those hitherto unpublished, only using official photographs for those prototype or extinct machines which the visitor has no chance of seeing.

A list of all the books, articles and papers consulted by the authors would cover several pages. Some of them are quoted in the text but we are also particularly indebted to the following works:

LOCOMOTIVES OF THE RAILWAYS OF THE SOVIET UNION
by V. A. Rakov, *in Russian*.
LOCOMOTIVE CONSTRUCTION AND DESIGN CALCULATIONS
by L. B. Yanush, W. M. Pansky and B. A. Pavlov,
in Russian and in German.

It is also a great pleasure to acknowledge the valuable help, freely given, in the provision of information, loan of books etc., preparation of drawings and permission to reproduce so many interesting photographs for which we wish to thank Messrs Beyer, Peacock & Co. Ltd, J. C. Cosgrave, A. E. Durrant, H. Fröhlich, W. H. C. Kelland, E. Konrad, R. G. Lewis (*Railway Age*), R. E. H. Mellor, J. O. Slezak, A. C. Sterndale, Dr J. Vial, A. G. Wells and the *Railway Gazette*. We are also most grateful to Mrs R. Le Fleming for checking and typing the manuscript and to L. S. K. Le Fleming for Russian translation and transcription.

In spite of our researches, however, the subject of Russian steam locomotives, like the Soviet Union itself, is so vast that there remain many gaps in our knowledge. The authors will be glad to hear from any reader who may be able to add to their information about locomotive class totals and the whereabouts of the locomotives concerned. We have indicated under the respective class headings the number-ranges in which further first hand observations are particularly desired. It would be satisfactory if one day a sequel could be published which, together with this book, would serve as a permanent complete work of reference on the Russian steam locomotive in the twentieth century. Although the building of main-line steam locomotives in Russia has ended, the work of gathering information about them has not. Perhaps it is also not too much to hope that many of the restrictions imposed on research into what is now a historical subject will be relaxed.

At the end of the book, notes on certain closely related aspects of the subject have been set out as appendices for the reader's easy reference. These are:

a. Russian railway titles. The purpose here is to give the different names under which certain trunk lines have been known, at various periods both before and after the Revolution.

b. Russian locomotive-building works.

c. Liveries of locomotives and rolling stock.

d. The Cyrillic alphabet with its transcription. In the text, engine class letters are given in the English transcription followed, at their first mention, by the Cyrillic letters in parenthesis.

The inclusion of a biography of Russian locomotive engineers is beyond the scope of this book, but many of the well-known names appear in the text. Enumeration of locomotive dimensions has been reduced to a bare minimum as they are now all available in other publications. Weights are given in metric tons (2,204 lb).

Note to This Edition

When this book was first published, in December 1960, its authors modestly made few claims as to its standard of authority or coverage, since wide areas of the U.S.S.R. were closed to visitors and little knowledge existed of the locomotives they harboured. However, the past twelve years have shown that their researches were in fact remarkably complete and accurate, and their work will stand as the definitive history of the steam locomotive in the U.S.S.R.

In this edition, the main text has been up-dated to mid-1971, but the historical and technical data contributed by the late H. M. Le Fleming (who died in November 1961) have been repeated in substantially their original form. To determine which classes of locomotive remain has not been easy, for the steam locomotive in Russia is living on borrowed time, the original intention having been to eliminate steam traction by the end of 1970. This plan was not fulfilled, and 2.7 per cent of Russia's train mileage was still steam-worked during 1971. To assist would-be visitors in locating the surviving steam locomotives, there is at the end of the book a map of the Soviet railways showing the principal means of traction on each line, based on *Geografiya Putej Soobshcheniya* by N. N. Kazanskiy (Moscow, 1969) and revised from later announcements.

No revised date has been given for the elimination of steam traction on the Russian railways, but the time cannot be far off. It will not, however, apply to the huge mileage of industrial and forestry railways, on which steam traction will probably survive long after it has disappeared from the mainline network.

March 1972   J. H. Price

Chapter 1

THE RUSSIAN STEAM LOCOMOTIVE

Before beginning our description of the different Russian locomotive types it will be useful to group together some general
characteristics and remarks. The first is that, with minor excep-
tions, the locomotives described in this book are the broad-gauge
stock of the main line railway system; the general remarks that
follow apply to these and not to the narrow gauge or industrial
types, which are dealt with separately.

The second is the widespread standardisation of locomotive
types. This is not a product of the Soviet planned economy; it
results rather from the sheer size of the unified railway system,
which has pursued a policy of standardisation for more than
eighty years. One of the first acts of the centralised administration
set up in Tsarist times was to order large numbers of a few
standard locomotive classes, and in the period since 1905 the total
of nine thousand locomotives in one class or group has been
exceeded twice, two other classes have approached or exceeded
the five thousand mark, three more have totalled about three
thousand and two others have exceeded two thousand. As a result,
a given type of work was generally performed by the same class of
locomotive practically throughout the U.S.S.R. Incidentally, this
book when published in its first edition caused some revision of
previous ideas on the world's largest classes of steam locomotive.

The principal factor in the geographical localisation of types
was the weight of rail, which permitted heavier locomotives to be
used only on those lines, known as 'trunk lines', which could
accept a higher-than-standard axle-loading. This explains, for
instance, why certain locomotive classes such as the Felix

Dzherzhinsky 2–10–2 and the equivalent 2–8–4 were found south of Moscow rather than north or west. Apart from this, the standardisation of types operated in favour of the visitor, for since every locomotive class was built in large numbers to perform a specific range of tasks, a depot handling a normal variety of work would usually have some of every class. The visitor of ten years ago who travelled by train on the tourist routes in Western Russia would thus see at least half of the standard locomotive types during his fortnight's or three weeks' tour, and a traveller by the Trans-Siberian Railway in 1958 saw only one locomotive class not also found in European Russia. At the time of writing, the best places to see steam locomotives would appear to be Latvia, Lithuania, Estonia, parts of Byelorussia, the Polish border (Western Ukraine) and the non-electrified portion of the Trans-Siberian Railway.

Another basic feature of Russia's locomotive stock is the great preponderance of freight locomotives. In 1955, a year in which the steam locomotive's share of traffic was still 86 per cent, 60 per cent of those in use were employed on freight trains, 20 per cent in shunting, 5 per cent on engineers' trains and other special duties, and only 15 per cent on passenger work. Of the thirty-six thousand steam locomotives which the authors believe to have existed at that time, no less than two-thirds were ten-coupled freight locomotives of the 0–10–0, 2–10–0 and 2–10–2 types, while passenger locomotives only numbered some four thousand. Fewer than one per cent of the total were tank locomotives, the overwhelming majority being tender engines.

The first thing about Russian locomotives that strikes the visitor is their great height. With a loading gauge reaching 17 ft 4⅝ in above rail level, engines 17 ft high are not uncommon. As this is about 4 ft higher than those in Britain, the effect is most impressive. The broader rail gauge, 5 ft 0 in (1524 mm) is not particularly noticeable, but the greater width of the rolling stock, up to 2 ft 6 in or more, comes as a pleasant suprise when settling down in a sleeping berth. Uniquely Russian is the railed-in engine platform on the older engines (see page 25).

Most Russian trains are not fast (passengers in a hurry can now go by air) and stops are lengthy, but engines and rolling stock are very clean and well kept – ideal conditions in fact for

18

the railway enthusiast (though travelling 'hard class' may prove unsavoury). There is often a holiday spirit about train travel. Russians seem to enjoy it and to have evolved a pleasant technique for journeys that may well last a week or more, since from Vladivostok to the Polish border by rail is over 6,300 miles.

In tracing Russian locomotive development many parallels with American practice will be found, particularly in the earliest and also the final stages. Tank engines, apart from small industrial and yard shunters, are rare, and since 1930 no engines with inside cylinders have been built. In both countries the loading gauge permits the use of motive power far larger than elsewhere and, for the largest designs, a preference has been shown for the Mallet over other articulated systems. This similarity is not altogether surprising with such analogous geographical conditions – vast distances, climatic extremes and an abundance of indigenous fuel: wood, coal and oil.

In pre-Revolutionary years over 50 per cent of the locomotives burnt oil, about 25 per cent coal and about 20 per cent wood. Wood-burning has gradually died out, whilst oil-burning was reduced as a matter of policy after 1928, only to be revived in recent years. Today, all surviving main line steam locomotives appear to be oil fired. Three men are sometimes seen on the foot-plate, not as a survival from wood-burning days, since the third man today is usually an apprentice. Air brakes of the Westinghouse pattern have become general since the 1890s. The automatic central coupler programme, begun in 1932, was due for completion in 1957, and freight engines and wagons are now to be seen without side buffers. The latter, however, are apparently being retained on passenger stock.

Cabs became general in the U.S.A. in the 1850s and no doubt the same was the case in Russia where the winter climate was even more severe. Engines without cabs can be seen in some early illustrations of imported machines, but it seems that they were fitted with them on arrival. Modern engines have totally enclosed cabs with tender shelters and, often, flexible bellows connections between them. The interiors are lined with wood to insulate them against the cold and keep out draughts, but this makes them rather dark. Since about 1932, therefore, clerestory roofs with small windows have been fitted to give extra light. Enormous oil head lamps, again reminiscent of America, were still a standard feature up to the late 1920s. For a short period thereafter the more compact Continental pattern was fitted, before the adoption of dynamo electric-lighting sets in the 1930s. The usual absence of cow catchers or pilots before the latter period may seem surprising, but no large unattended herds of cattle roamed the countryside as in the U.S.A.; however, when the present writer's wife crossed the Trans-Siberian Railway in 1915, a cow *was* run over and caused delay to the train. In addition to the usual chime whistle a deep-toned klaxon is now fitted to larger passenger locomotives, adding a new and striking note to the familiar railway sounds.

A surprising feature of the Russian railways, at least until very recently, was the number of very old locomotives still to be found. Mr P. E. Garbutt, in his book *The Russian Railways* (1949), makes the point that in 1941 more than half the total Soviet locomotive stock consisted of engines less than twelve years old, which gave the U.S.S.R. the right to claim its locomotive stock as the youngest in the world. However, the remainder included a great many pre-Revolutionary machines, retained in service because the new engines were almost all absorbed by the demands of increasing freight traffic.

In determining which classes still exist we have used first hand reports for the most part, but have also taken into account a Russian work by A. P. Micheyev, which set out the standard classes existing in 1953 according to their power classification.

TYPE OF TRAFFIC	HEAVY DUTIES	MEDIUM DUTIES	LIGHT DUTIES
Freight	FD, L	SO, E, Ye, 52	Sh,a
	(ФД, Л)	(СО, Э, Е, 52)	(ШᴬA)
Passenger	IS	Su, Sum, S	B, Ku
	(ИС)	(Сᵞ, Сᵞᴹ, С)	(Б, Кᵞ)
Engineers' Trains and Transfer Trips	—	Mr, Shch	N
		(Мᵖ, Щ)	(Н)
Shunting	—	E (Э)	O
		for hump yards	

To these must now be added LV (ЛВ) for heavy freight and P36 (П36) for heavy passenger duties.

This list does not include all the classes known to exist in quantity – A. P. Micheyev himself states that there are twenty-five such classes, and a more extensive list is given in chapter 11 – but in addition to confirming the existence of several Tsarist locomotive classes it is of interest as an official statement of steam locomotive power ratings. There does not appear to be any more detailed system of power classification such as that in Britain, but the concentration on a few standard types of locomotive probably makes this unnecessary.

Here should also be described the numbering system, which plays a large part in assessing the class totals. Russian locomotives are numbered separately by classes, and not in a single series as in Britain or Finland, nor by railway regions. In 1912, soon after the unification of the principal Russian railways was completed, the well-known railway engineer, C. V. Lomonosov, drew up a new locomotive numbering scheme to replace those of the former companies and administrations, each class taking the initial letter of some name or word connected with it, such as the initial of the builder, the designer or the railway (e.g. the standard 0–8–0 goods locomotive became Class O, the O denoting *Osnovnoi*, or 'principal'). This system of class letters is still in force today for most locomotives, though from 1931 onwards two letters were frequently used for new classes, instead of one.

When standard locomotives are built in large numbers over a period of several years there are almost certain to be detail differences between the various batches. This is the case in Russia, and the sub-classes are denoted by a 'cipher', a small letter which follows the locomotive's main class letter. This can best be illustrated by an example: the 0–10–0 freight design of 1912 received class letter E, a batch of generally similar locomotives built in Germany in 1921–3 became sub-class Eg, a modernised version of 1931 became class Em, and a condensing version of this later variety became class Emk. The locomotive number was however in a single series for the whole of class E, and would remain unchanged even if the locomotive was rebuilt to a different sub-class. This absence of any renumbering since 1912 has naturally assisted the authors not a little in their assessment of class totals. Most of the sub-class indices, or ciphers, are explained in the text, but we have deliberately omitted the many sub-classes of some older engines, whose inclusion would add unnecessarily to the length of the book. In these cases the 1912 classification is used, except where the class became extinct before that date.

The number of a Russian locomotive appears on the sides of the cab and is usually (though not always) repeated on the buffer beam and on the back of the tender. The number is usually painted in cream, although certain locomotives have it in raised metal letters. Above it is the red, green and yellow badge of the Russian railways, with the letters U.S.S.R. (C.C.C.P.) above and crossed hammers below, occasionally with the additional letters 'M.P.S.' (М.П.С.), standing for 'Ministry of Ways of Communications'. The badge is flanked by the abbreviation of the railway division to which the locomotive is allocated: thus, ОКТ. Ж.Д. is the abbreviation for Октябрьская железная дорога or 'October Railway'. This is the railway division comprising the Moscow–Leningrad main line and other lines around Leningrad; a list of some of the present railway divisions and their abbreviations appears in Appendix I. As on most large systems, tenders are often changed, so that a number noted on the back of the tender is not necessarily also that of the engine to which it is coupled.

Chapter 2

LOCOMOTIVE DEVELOPMENT UNDER
THE TSARS 1833-1916

Before 1914 many isolated articles and papers on Russian locomotives appeared in the technical press. Usually confined to one
batch of an engine class only, and widely scattered in British,
French, American and German periodicals, they did not make it
possible to gain a comprehensive view of this fascinating subject.
Now that a more complete summary can be made it will be seen
that many interesting and unusual engines were built, whilst other
types, which one might have expected to find, were conspicuous by
their absence in what has been almost *terra incognita* to the enthusiast for many years.

The aim of this chapter is to give a brief historical review of
Russian locomotive development from 1833 to 1917, with the
background factors that shaped its course, and at the same time to
pick out for the connoisseur the more unusual designs or their
component features. Some duplication with chapter 3 is unavoid-
able, and the reader who is in a hurry to make the acquaintance of
present-day Russian locomotives can turn at once to page 34.

In 1833 the first Russian steam locomotive was constructed at
Nizhni-Tagil in the Urals by M. Cherepanov, who had just visited
England and seen Stephenson's and other early locomotives at
work. It ran on a track of about half a mile in length, laid to 5 ft
6 in (1670 mm) gauge. Pictures of a model of this engine have been
somewhat touched up but it can be seen to have had four small
wheels of equal diameter with inside frames and cylinders. As there
is no sign of coupling rods it may be assumed to have been a 2-2-0.
A second and larger engine was begun but funds ran out before it
could be completed.

The first railway was the 14-mile line from St Petersburg to Tsarskoe Selo. Laid to 6 ft (1830 mm) gauge, it was opened to horse-drawn traffic in 1836, and to steam in October 1837 when the first locomotive, a Hawthorn 2–2–0, arrived from England. Additional locomotives were two Stephenson 2–2–2s, an engine from Cockerill (Belgium) and two others, probably 'Sharpies' standard 2–2–2s similar to those on the G.N.R. in England. Speeds up to 40 m.p.h. were reached, and two trucks of sand were thoughtfully provided next to the engine for the reception of passengers, who, it was believed, would become air-borne in the event of a sudden stop.

Russia's second railway, the Warsaw-Vienna, was built in 1845–8 and conformed to the standard gauge, 4 ft 8½ in (1435 mm) already in use in Austria. During this period William and Octavius Norris of Philadelphia were building locomotives in Vienna and the introduction of the American type 4–4–0 had great influence on early Central European development. Another Philadelphia firm, Eastwick & Harrison, had, in 1839, produced the famous American 4–4–0 'Gowan and Marx', an engine that greatly impressed the Russians, the aptness of the name having however no significance at that time! This company built up such a good trade with Russia that it later closed down in Philadelphia and opened up in that country. Amongst locomotives supplied were some 0–6–0s in the early 1840s. These proving heavy at the front end, carrying axles were added, producing thereby the earliest examples of the 2–6–0 wheel arrangement.

Meanwhile, in 1843, work had been started on the first Russian trunk line, from St Petersburg to Moscow. A gauge of 5 ft 0 in (1524 mm) was decided upon and henceforward became standard for Russian main lines. The Alexandrovsky works outside St Petersburg were taken over by the State for the manufacture of railway equipment, and the line was opened to traffic throughout in 1851. Direction of these works was put in the hands of Ross Winans and his partners, of Baltimore & Ohio fame, a connection which, with one break, lasted until 1869, by which time locomotive production at these works, after the completion of two hundred and twenty-five engines, had become intermittent.

Principal types turned out at Alexandrovsky were 0–6–0s, 0–8–0s and 4–4–0s. Some of the latter, proving heavy at the front end, had additional carrying axles added, thus creating the rare 6–4–0 wheel arrangement. The earliest 0–8–0s, built in 1858, were the first eight-coupled engines in Russia. American influence, so noticeable in many early engines of the period, was thus clearly established.

Other railways were begun, linking important centres, and radiating from St Petersburg, Moscow, Kursk, Riga, etc., the total mileage reaching 12,500 by 1879. Some of these lines were hastily constructed, the Moscow-Kursk for example earning the sobriquet of 'The Bone-breaker' on account of frequent accidents. In fairness however, it must be remembered that the Russian engineers were up against a formidable climatic factor, scarcely found elsewhere. The intense cold of the winter freezes the ground to a great depth, causing expansion of moisture-bearing subsoil, which may severely distort the road bed and track, whilst the Spring thaw also has its dangers.

From 1860 to 1890, the ever-growing demand for locomotives could not be met from Russian building capacity and many classes were delivered by British, French, German and Austrian firms. Amongst the former were Stephenson, Kitson, Sharp Stewart and Beyer Peacock. Types supplied were chiefly 2–4–0s, 0–6–0s and 0–8–0s, with a fair number of 0–4–2s. Nearly all had inside frames with outside cylinders, but some 0–6–0s of Austrian and German build had outside frames and cylinders whilst those of Belgian origin were of the Belpaire pattern, with outside frames and inside cylinders.

In addition to such orthodox machines were four 4–2–0 Cramptons, supplied by Cail (France) in 1861, which were not finally withdrawn until 1905. In 1862 two double-framed 2–4–2s with cylinders between the inner and outer frames were delivered by Schneider (France). Some lack of imagination was shown by these builders in providing only spectacle plates as protection against the Russian climate, a defect remedied by the provision of large cabs after their arrival. Even the Tsar, Alexander II, was more concerned with the enginemen's welfare for, in the early 1870s, a decree was issued by him that the platforms of all locomotives were to be railed in to prevent men falling from the slippery surfaces when these were iced over, or when suddenly running into winter track distortion. This 'promenade deck' effect was for many years a

Russian characteristic and remains a unique feature of the older and middle-aged locomotives in the U.S.S.R. Two further engines similar to the Schneider 2–4–2s were built in Russia in 1869–70.

In 1870 a roving Russian commission was favourably impressed by the Fairlie locomotive and five 0–6/6–0s of this type were built by Sharp Stewart for a minor 3 ft 6 in gauge railway. From 1872 onward broad gauge 'Fairlies' of the same wheel arrangement were built for sections of the Trans-Caucasian Railway. Makers included Avonside, Sharp Stewart, the Yorkshire Engine Co. and Sigl (Vienna), whilst later engines were turned out at Kolomna in the 1880s. Various batches differed in detail, as was later denoted by the class suffix. Converted from wood to oil-burning, with fuel tanks over the boiler barrels in turn surmounted by transverse air reservoirs, they bore a strong resemblance to pack-horses (*pl. 16, 17*). Of the forty-five engines built, forty-three survived to be renumbered F (Ф) 9800–42, in 1912. In 1924–6 they were transferred to the Rioni-Tvkibuli line and its branches, where they put in a further ten years' service.

Kolomna built some interesting 2–6–0s in 1878, which were classed 'A'. With 5 ft 0 in coupled wheels they were claimed to be the first purely passenger 'Moguls'. They had rocking grates, a useful feature overlooked until revived on some 0–10–0s built at the same works in 1915. The year 1880 saw the introduction of the first compound, a Russian South Western Railway locomotive having been converted to the Mallet two-cylinder system by Alexander Borodin, then Engineer-in-Chief of the railway.

The first experiments with oil-burning on locomotives in Russia took place in 1876, but to Thomas Urquhart, Locomotive Superintendent of the Gryaze & Tsaritsyn Railway in S. E. Russia, must be given the credit for its first really successful application. By the end of 1884 he had all his one hundred and forty-three engines running on petroleum refuse and had also perfected a firebox to burn wood and oil simultaneously. By 1890 there were over one thousand oil-burning locomotives in Russia and others in Rumania. Urquhart was also a pioneer of compounding, converting engines to his own two-cylinder system from 1887 onwards (*pl. 5*).

The Russo-Turkish War of 1877–8 brought to light many shortcomings in the railway system, as a result of which a special Commission on Railway Affairs was appointed, its recommendations being subsequently carried out by the Ministry of Ways of Communication. Amongst these recommendations were:

1. Acceleration of the purchase of private railways by the State. In pursuance of this policy about one third of the total mileage became State-owned by 1894 and about two thirds by 1912.
2. Development of a large additional locomotive building capacity in Russia, to reduce imports. Works at Bryansk, Nevsky, Putilov, Kharkov, Sormovo and Lugansk all began to turn out locomotives in the 1890s.
3. Reduction of the very large number of locomotive classes by the adoption of standard basic designs suitable for general use, so that economic bulk orders could be placed. Such engines were referred to as 'Government Stock' or 'State Reserve'. It was also recommended that the 0–6–0 type be discontinued for main line freight.

One of the first of these standard classes was the Ch (Ч) 0–8–0 (*pl. 4*). Built between 1879 and 1892, many of the later examples were compounds on the plan of E. E. Noltein, then Engineer-in-Chief of the Moscow-Kazan Railway. Some of them survived until 1935. Their successors were the ubiquitous O Class (see chapter 3), some of which are still to be seen. They originated in an order for thirty 0–8–0 compounds designed by V. I. Lopushinsky for the Far-Caucasian Railway in 1889, which design was adopted as a basic standard. Construction continued right up to the 1920s, the total eventually exceeding nine thousand engines, divided into about eight sub-classes.

By 1890 the old American type 4–4–0s were no longer sufficiently powerful for main-line passenger work, and this was given as one of the contributory causes of a crash involving a Tsar's train which was double-headed. A new design, capable of working 390-ton trains at 50 m.p.h. was ordered, its design being worked out by Professor N. L. Shchukin in collaboration with A. Belpaire of Belgian State Railway fame. Hence, no doubt, the choice of the 2–6–0 type. The first examples of this N (H) Class appeared in 1892 as compounds with Joy's valve gear. Built in large numbers up to 1912 (see chapter 3), they became the most universal passenger class until superseded by the S class 2–6–2s. A similar class Ya (Я), *pl. 11*, did not last as long as the 'N's.

The beginning of the 1890 decade also saw the re-introduction of the 4–4–0 type in modern form, followed by the first 4–6–0s in 1891 and the first 2–8–0s in 1895, whilst the building of numerous 0–8–0s continued. An unusual feature of many of these engines built between 1891 and 1912 (as well as some 0–6–0s and some Tanks) was the earlier form of outside Joy valve gear. In this the connecting link, the anchor link and the piercing of the connecting rod were eliminated and replaced by a return crank and rod.

In 1891 a notable tandem compound 4–4–0 was built by the Société Alsacienne at Belfort at the instigation of A. Borodin and in collaboration with A. de Glehn and A. Mallet. Classed Pb (Пб), it ran on the Russian S. W. Railway, which built six similar engines at its Odessa works in 1894–5. The success of these engines led to a State Railway order for sixty-eight units, of an enlarged and improved Class Pp (Пп), being placed on the Putilov works. They were delivered in 1898–1900, at about the same time as the slightly smaller Class Pr (Пр) were being turned out at Kolomna. These 4–4–0s had a life of twenty-five to thirty years. At the same time tandem compound freight engines, the 2–8–0s of Class R (Р), were put in hand (pl. 22). Inside Allan valve gear was fitted. Between 1899 and 1910 some three hundred were built at Bryansk, Putilov, Sormovo and by foreign firms, thus forming the largest class of such engines in existence. Vauclain compounds from the Baldwin Locomotive Works (U.S.A.) were represented by the Class Kh (Х) 2–8–0s of 1895, the Class V (В) 4–6–0s of 1896 and a pair of 2–10–0s, Yef (ЕФ), for trial against the 'Fairlies' on the Trans-Caucasian.

In 1895 the first Russian articulated Mallet compound tender locomotives were put into service on the 3 ft 6 in gauge Vologda–Archangel Railway. They were 0–6/6–0s, as were the broad gauge engines built in Russia from 1897 for the Moscow–Kazan Railway. The drawbar pull of these early Mallets sometimes exceeded the strength of the wagon couplings, which necessitated some unusual equipment. Mounted on the sides of the tender frames were compressed air cylinders linked to cables by which the rear half of the train could be independently coupled up (pl. 18). The wire ropes were guided by pulley brackets on the sides of the intervening wagons.

Work on the Trans-Siberian Railway began in 1890, the Western section being opened in 1896, the Central section in 1899 and the Eastern line to Vladivostok in 1902. Lake Baikal, however, still had to be crossed by ferry. During the Russo-Japanese War of 1904–5 this gap was a great handicap – at one time twenty-five miles of track were temporarily laid on ice! The difficult rail link round the South end of the lake was pushed forward to completion in 1905. Thirty-eight tunnels were necessary on one stretch of forty-two miles.

For mountainous stretches (ruling grade 1 in 57) of this immense undertaking Mallet tender engines were put into service from 1903 onwards. Passenger traffic was hauled by 2–4/4–0s of Class I (Ï, obsolete letter), about one hundred of which were eventually built. Some of them, like the freight engines described below, were built as simples with four high pressure cylinders, much to Anatole Mallet's displeasure, it is said. For freight work Class Ph (Θ, obsolete letter) 0–6/6–0s were used, about three hundred and fifty being built between 1903 and 1916 (*pl. 18*). An interesting variant was built at Kolomna in 1910. This was a simple, with both sets of cylinders placed at the centre in order to simplify the steam piping. It was not repeated; nor were similar engines, tried in other countries at this time, a success. The orthodox 0–6/6–0s were transferred to the Central Asian Railway in 1930 but were evidently displaced from these lines by more modern machines a few years later.

Russian engines were being built with superheaters as early as 1902 and, about this period, an old 0–8–0 was fitted with a Brotan semi-water-tube boiler that, however, did not find favour. Various superheaters were designed by Russian engineers, but only those by Notkin, Niemeyer and Chusov were adopted to any great extent.

Main line tank engines were rare but, although few in number, were so distinctive as to be noteworthy. In 1904 some four-cylinder compound 4–6–2 tanks were built for the Ryazan–Ural Railway with all four cylinders driving the leading coupled axle. Further engines with superheaters followed in 1906, but the third batch, of 1907–09, were quite unique 'semi-tanks'. With very short side tanks for oil fuel alongside the firebox, they had totally enclosed cabs and small six-wheel tenders for water only. In spite of their odd appearance the arrangement was most suitable for the climatic conditions (*pl. 14*). They were designed by Prof. A. S. Raevsky, the leading exponent of multi-cylinder engines in Russia. Of a slightly earlier period were some 2–6–2 Ts with normal side tanks, others with tanks very shallow at the sides (the main part being between the frames), and 4–6–0 Ts with very long side tanks, sometimes even extending across the front of the smokebox. Much more pleasing in appearance were the (hard sign)n (Ъⁿ) Class 2–8–2 Ts of 1910, in which the tank assembly was accommodated between the frames and the rather high-pitched boiler, the flat tank top forming the engine platform. On the suburban services for which they were built they could handle 480-ton trains at 47 m.p.h.

The larger passenger tender engines built during the first decade of the century were 4–6–0s. Class G (Г) of 1900 were two-cylinder compounds driving on the leading coupled axle. Re-built in 1909–13 as superheated simples, they were sent to the Far-Caucasian and Chinese Eastern Railways. Class U (У), constructed between 1903 and 1910, were four-cylinder de Glehn compounds. In 1912 two larger superheated engines, classed Uᵘ (Уу), were completed and were the last 'de Glehns' and the last compound passenger engines to be built in Russia. By 1940 the survivors had been relegated to minor branch lines, but G 127, which drew Lenin's funeral train in 1924, is preserved at the Paveletsky Station in Moscow. Another 4–6–0, which hauled the train bearing Lenin on his arrival in Russia in 1917, was presented to the U.S.S.R. by Finland, in 1957 (No. 293 of the Finland State Railway). The K series (chapter 3), dating from 1908, were two cylinder simples with 5 ft 7 in coupled wheels. Some of them bore a strong resemblance to the Prussian P8s, but with much higher-pitched boilers, the highest (at 10 ft 6 in) in Russia at that time. Two were fitted with special valves and Savelyov valve gear of the Belpaire type, with motion derived from the crossheads. In 1910 the first of the S Class 2–6–2s came out and thereafter steadily replaced all these 4–6–0s as well as those of earlier classes.

Contemporary freight engines were represented by the numerous Shch (Щ) Class 2–8–0s (chapter 3, *pl. 24*). In addition to the usual variants, compound and simple, saturated and superheated, individual units were the subjects of many trials and experiments, one being fitted, as late as 1944, with a boiler having a stay-less corrugated firebox. Between 1927 and 1934, three hundred were completely reconstructed and classed Shch, ch (Щ ч).

30

By 1906 the need for a more powerful engine was apparent and E. E. Noltein got out a design for an 0–8–0 with a 16-ton axle load. Introduced in 1908, and classed Hy (V, obsolete letter), they were employed chiefly on shunting. Somewhat similar engines with a 15-ton axle load were classed Y (Ы), three hundred and fifty being built during the period 1909–16. Their compound variants were the most powerful in Russia. Both classes were modern in appearance, resembling a shortened version of the 0–10–0s which superseded all these eight-coupled engines after 1912. It seems unlikely that such useful and comparatively modern engines should have all disappeared and many may well be still employed on industrial branches. Built on the same lines were the light 2–8–0s of Class I (И), 1909–11, with an axle load of 13·9 tons. These were all going strong in 1936 but, as with other numerically small classes, subsequent references to them have been omitted from published returns.

Around 1910, Stumpf uniflow cylinders were applied to locomotives, Kolomna works being the first to turn out an engine with them: a Hy Class 0–8–0. The following year they built four 2–6–0s (two superheated and two saturated) of the large group N (H) and a narrow gauge 0–8–0 (shown at the Turin Exhibition), all with uniflow cylinders. In 1913–14 these were also fitted to eleven narrow gauge tank engines as replacements, and to five broad gauge 0–10–0s, but the outbreak of war put an end to further progress.

No doubt those interested in locomotives will often have been struck by the almost complete absence in Russia of the 4–4–2, 4–6–2 and 2–8–2 types. So common elsewhere, this group was represented by only sixty-six 'Pacifics' of Class L (Л), described in chapter 3. The two main reasons for their absence were the height of the loading gauge, which allowed coupled wheels to be placed beneath large fireboxes (rendering trailing trucks inessential) and, after 1910, the wide adoption of the 2–6–2 and 0–10–0 types. The 2–6–2 became the principal standard passenger engine for forty years (1911 to 1951) in contrast to other countries, where its vogue was shorter and its scope much more limited.

This famous S (C) Class originated as a Ministerial project of March 1908, specifying a 2–6–2 with a Krauss truck at the front end, a boiler with a large coal-burning grate and a Notkin superheater. Provision was also to be made for variation of the axle load by adjustments to the leading truck and spring gear, whilst the wheel base was to be kept as short as possible – a point which ruled out the 'Pacific' type. Designed and built at Sormovo – hence the designation, S class – the first five engines were turned out at the end of 1910. The story of these engines is continued in later chapters (3 and 4), but one interesting branch of the family may be mentioned here: the standard gauge Sv (C^B) Class built for the Warsaw–Vienna line. Cut down in height, with flared chimneys and straight platforms, only the railings on the latter showed their Russian origin. One of the last of the pre-1917 designs, fifteen of them were built in 1915. Subsequently converted to 5 ft gauge and to oil-burning, they worked between Moscow and Kursk. In 1945 they were transferred to the Byelo-Russian Railway and worked there until withdrawal.

Having seen how a happy solution to the all-round passenger-engine problem was found we must now turn to the freight engine situation, which was far from satisfactory. As early as 1905 various railways began to press for a ten-coupled engine, as the 2–8–0s were becoming inadequate for the increasing loads. The authorities however were very cautious, the numerous designs submitted being modified out of all recognition by various committees, and finally shelved. After the buck had been adroitly passed around for six years the first E (Э) Class 0–10–0s eventually emerged in 1912. The design that actually materialised was largely the work of V. I. Lopushinsky and the Lugansk works, where the engines were built. As oil-burners for the Far-Caucasus they had $23\frac{5}{8}$ in diameter cylinders and were later classed E^{L1} (Эл1). These were followed by coal-burners, with cylinders enlarged to $24\frac{3}{4}$ in, for the Northern Donetz line, Class E^{L2} (Эл2). Their success leading to full State approval in 1915 – but with cylinders further enlarged to $25\frac{9}{16}$ in – production of the standard class E began in the principal locomotive works and, as could have been said only a few years ago, has continued ever since (see chapters 3 and 4).

This class not only eventually reached the largest total in the world but also, the Russians claim, was in more or less continuous production for a longer period than any other single basic design. Looking back, therefore, bureaucracy's long reluctance to accept it can be viewed with some amusement, and no doubt its sponsors had many subsequent opportunities of saying 'I told you so!' In Russia at that time a 16-ton axle load was generally permissible, whilst wagon couplings could take a pull of up to 16 tons. A ten-coupled engine could therefore produce a drawbar pull of this amount with an ample factor of adhesion and margin of power.

One of the more intriguing locomotive mysteries of World War I concerned some Flamme four-cylinder 2–10–0s of the Belgian State Railway. In 1914 a considerable number were under construction and subsequent examination of makers' lists showed that many more of these engines had been built than could be seen in Belgium after the war. It transpired that, early in the war, eighty of them were transferred by the Central Powers to Galicia in N. E. Austria, to work behind the Eastern Front. Captured in a Russian offensive, they were converted to 5 ft gauge and sent to the Catherine Railway, the first going into service at the end of 1915. In Russia they were classed F (Φ), for Flamme, retaining their Belgian numbers in the 44xx series and thus not clashing with the 'Fairlies' numbered in the 98xxs.

In 1915 a purchasing commission to acquire railway equipment, including two thousand locomotives, in the U.S.A. was set up under the direction of Professor N. L. Shchukin and G. V. Lomonosov (who later became a pioneer of large diesel locomotives). Most numerous of these American engines were the Ye (E) Class 2–10–0s described in the next chapter, delivery of which was not fully completed owing to the political situation. Another uncompleted order was for 3 ft 6 in gauge 0–6/6–0 Mallets of Class a (a), a modern version of the Vologda–Archangel type mentioned on page 28. They were ordered in 1916, but by the time the first were completed, heavy wartime traffic had made it necessary to convert the whole railway to 5 ft. gauge. Those left on the makers' hands (some being converted to metre gauge) eventually found their way to various parts of the world, for instance Malaya, where the present writer was very familiar with two of them.

Preparation of a new locomotive design seems to have been a pleasant business in Russia. It was usually entrusted to an eminent authority who had often been both chief engineer of a railway and professor of Railway Engineering at a university and was free to collaborate with others, including foreigners. After approval, production details were worked out with the staff of the works where the prototypes were to be built.

Chapter 3

PRE-REVOLUTIONARY CLASSES
IN SERVICE IN 1960

Class O (RUSSIAN **O**) *pl. 6–9, 72*

The oldest steam locomotives to survive in recent years in the Soviet Union, and the oldest class still in limited use, are the long-boilered 0–8–0 goods locomotives of Class O. This class, as we have seen, dates back to 1889, a few years later an improved version being adopted as standard by a number of railways and built by at least seven different builders up to about 1900. In the locomotive numbering scheme of 1912 these locomotives received class letter O, the O denoting *Osnovnoi Tip* (principal or basic type). Their sub-class cipher was d to denote their Joy valve gear, this name appearing in Cyrillic as approximately *Dzhoi*. Several hundred Od 0–8–0s were built, and a few examples remained in industrial service into the 1960s.

The Od locomotives were soon far outnumbered, however, by their successors, the Ov (Ob) type of 1901 in which the b (pronounced v) denotes that they have Walschaerts valve gear. These two-cylinder compound 0–8–0s were chosen as Russia's standard goods-locomotives during the period of the unification of the railways, and were built continuously by all the main builders from 1901 until 1909, with further batches later. When numbered into the O series in 1912 they brought the total for the class up to about eight thousand, increased by later additions to a grand total of almost exactly nine thousand by 1923 when the last few appeared, although by this time a number had been lost to Poland by the transfer of territory. The highest-numbered O Class locomotive noted by observers is 8,934. Those taken over by Poland were converted to standard gauge and one of these, removed by the Germans in 1945, was observed lying derelict at Nuremberg in 1952.

Although built for freight traffic, the O Class 0–8–0s have during their long lives passed through almost the entire range of jobs that a railway has to offer. George Behrend's book, *The History of Wagons-Lits*, shows one of them hauling the Trans-Siberian Express across the Steppes in 1900, and during the early years of the Revolution they were often used on passenger trains because there was nothing else available. Not until 1925 were they displaced in any numbers from main-line freight work, but then they found a new lease of life on shunting duties, and the survivors were all used on this work or for short freight transfer trips around factory estates or docks. It is difficult to form an accurate estimate of the number that survived to 1960, but examples of Ob locomotives were noted by observers during 1958–59 in the 2xxx, 3xxx, 4xxx, 5xxx, 6xxx and 7xxx series, with several higher-numbered 7xxx locomotives of a slightly different sub-class known as Ok. This may have been a rebuilding, for another Ok observed was locomotive Ok 124, seen freshly painted at Kasatin workshops.

There were also some other sub-classes, such as the 1923 locomotives which received the cipher u (for *usilenny*, strengthened, reinforced or more powerful). Although the numbers of the O class 0–8–0s are dwindling now, they outlived more modern types and many could be seen with tenders transferred from other scrapped locomotives, tenders often so large that they towered above the locomotive's own cab. One rarely passed a marshalling yard without seeing one or two of these handy veterans, and observers have reckoned that there were about twelve hundred of them left in 1959. Their survival was largely due to the comparatively late introduction of the diesel shunter in Russia. As the earliest pre-Revolutionary class still in general use they made a quaint contrast with the modern locomotives, and when a Russian journalist wrote about the railway modernisation plan he (or she) often used an O-class picture to denote the Locomotive of Yesterday. In 1959, *Pravda* even published a poetic tribute to locomotive Ov 7024, a citation for long service and meritorious conduct.

DIMENSIONS

Cylinders 19$\frac{11}{16}$ in. (19$\frac{11}{16}$ in. and 28$\frac{11}{16}$ in. compound) × 25$\frac{9}{16}$ in. *Coupled wheels* 3 ft 11$\frac{1}{4}$ in. dia. *Boiler pressure* 156 to 213 p.s.i. *Grate area* 19.9 ft². *Weight full (engine only)* 52 to 55 tons. *Max. axle load* 13$\frac{1}{2}$ tons.

Class Shch (RUSSIAN Щ) *pl. 23–25*

In 1905 the Ministry of Railways commissioned Professors N. L. Shchukin and A. S. Raevsky to design a new main-line freight locomotive of greater tractive effort than the Class O, and the result was a 2–8–0 goods locomotive, placed in service in 1907 on the Catherine, Moscow-Kursk and Southern railways, which in the 1912 reclassification was named Class Shch (Щ) in honour of its designer. This 2-cylinder compound design was built in large numbers in the 1910–1912 period. The total at the 1912 reclassification was one thousand eight hundred and fifty locomotives, but later construction up to 1918 increased this figure to about two thousand two hundred, perhaps more. Between 1927 and 1934, three hundred of them were rebuilt and classed Shch,ch (Щч).

Being less suitable for downgrading to shunting duties than the versatile O Class 0–8–0, the Shch Class 2–8–0s have almost disappeared, at least from Western Russia, and only three examples had been reported by visitors in 1957–59. It is probable, however, that many more were still at work in the areas beyond the usual tourist routes, especially the 1927–34 rebuilds. Those noted in Western Russia were of the un-rebuilt type such as numbers 810, 1035 and 1573, so there were probably between five hundred and one thousand still at work. Their 15 to 16-ton axle load made them especially useful for lightly-laid lines and they were shown in the official classification as 'medium-powered locomotives suitable for freight duties'.

DIMENSIONS
Cylinders 23$\frac{3}{16}$ in. (21$\frac{1}{4}$ in. and 30 in. compound) × 27$\frac{9}{16}$ in. *Coupled wheels* 4 ft 3$\frac{3}{16}$ in. dia. *Boiler pressure* 199 p.s.i. *Grate area* 30 ft². *Weight full (engine only)* 77 to 78 tons. *Max. axle load* 15 to 16 tons.

Class N (RUSSIAN H) *pl. 10, 12*

Before the advent of the Class S 2–6–2, one of the most widespread passenger locomotive types in Russia was the Class N 2–6–0, a large-wheeled type built between 1892 and 1913 to a total of about one thousand engines, which in 1912 received the classification N (for Nikolai Railway, for which they were first designed and built). There were very many variations according to the whims of different builders and railway divisions, giving thirteen different sub-classes in all. The axle load was between $14\frac{1}{2}$ and 16 tons according to the sub-class, and even after the larger 2–6–0s were in general use on most lines the Class N 2–6–0s still reigned supreme so far as passenger trains were concerned on many lightly-laid lines, including the long Turksib line from Novosibirsk to Tashkent, to which many of them were drafted.

Of the total number built, about half were withdrawn before 1939, leaving some five hundred in use, most of which had gone by 1955. Fewer than half-a-dozen had been noted by observers during 1958–9, and most of those were lying 'dead' at the back of roundhouses, although one of the authors saw one resplendent in green and crimson, in 1959. It is possible that some few may have been retained for such light duties as officers' specials, for there is no evidence that more than a few dozen of the class survived.

DIMENSIONS

Cylinders $21\frac{1}{4}$ in. $(21\frac{1}{4}$ in. and $29\frac{1}{2}$ in. compound$)$ × $25\frac{9}{16}$ in. *Coupled wheels* 5 ft 7 in. to 6 ft 3 in. dia. *Boiler pressure* 171 to 199 p.s.i. *Grate area* 23·6 to 28 ft². *Weight full (engine only)* 54 to 62 tons. *Max. axle load* $14\frac{1}{2}$ to 16 tons.

Class B (RUSSIAN Б) *pl. 19*

Among the locomotive classes still at work listed by a Russian publication in 1954 was the 4–6–0 Class B, though none have been noted by observers in Western Russia. The Class B 4–6–0, named from the Briansk Works where the design was evolved, numbered some two hundred and fifty locomotives built between 1908 and 1913, and until displaced by the Class S 2–6–2 in the late 1920s, these machines handled the principal passenger trains on the main lines from Moscow to Brest, Kursk, Voronesh and on some of the southern lines. They were then transferred to Central Asia, and a considerable number were also in service in Latvia between the Wars.

DIMENSIONS

Cylinders $21\frac{5}{8}$ × $27\frac{9}{16}$ in. *Coupled wheels* 6 ft 0 in. dia. *Boiler pressure* 185 p.s.i. *Grate area* 30 ft². *Weight full (engine only)* $74\frac{1}{2}$ tons. *Max. axle load* 15·7 tons.

Class Ku (RUSSIAN Ку) *pl. 21*

In 1907–9 a new class of 4–6–0 passenger engines was delivered to the Moscow-Kazan Railway. Built at Kolomna and the Putilov works, they were later classed K. A more powerful version, the Ku, followed from Kolomna in 1911–13, bringing the total up to some three hundred engines, most of which were to be found on the Moscow-Kazan line and Moscow suburban services. These were the last 4–6–0s to be produced in Russia, owing to the success of the 2–6–2s. After electrification they were dispersed to Siberia and the Far East and, although the two classes were intact in 1939, the older K class had disappeared by 1954, leaving the Ku engines at work.

DIMENSIONS
Cylinders 22⅝ × 25⅟₁₆ in. *Coupled wheels* 6 ft 2¾ in. dia. *Boiler pressure* 185 p.s.i. *Grate area* 34·2 ft². *Weight full (engine only)* 73 to 75 tons. *Max. axle load* 16 to 17 tons.

Class S (RUSSIAN C) *pl. 33*

Among the most successful locomotive designs ever produced in Russia was the Class S 2–6–2, the mainstay for the last thirty years of all passenger services other than the heaviest main line expresses. This class of more than three thousand locomotives had its origin in the 2–6–2 design produced in 1910 by the Sormovo works for the main lines radiating from Leningrad. According to V. A. Rakov about nine hundred Class S locomotives were built between 1911 and 1918, although almost all those seen latterly in Western Russia bore numbers below S350.

Almost all these machines existed in 1960, including some of the very first batch such as S 12 and S 28, and a small stud of them was kept to haul the international trains between Leningrad and the Finnish frontier at Vainikkala. Designed and first built at Sormovo (hence S Class), some of the later engines came from other builders such as Kolomna. The visitor who entered Russia via Finland would usually meet a Class S as his first Russian locomotive.

The later batches of Class S, with longer wheelbase, dating from 1926 to 1951, will be dealt with in chapter 4.

Cylinders 21⅝ × 27⁹⁄₁₆ in. *Coupled wheels* 6 ft 0 in. dia. *Boiler pressure* 185 p.s.i. *Grate area* 40·8 ft². *Weight full (engine only)* 75·8 tons. *Max. axle load* 15·8 tons.

Class E (RUSSIAN Э) *pl. 27*

The Class E 0–10–0, like the Class S 2–6–2, is a locomotive design produced in large numbers during the Soviet period but originating before 1918. In this case it is less easy to separate pre-Revolutionary from post-1918 machines, since production of the pre-1918 design continued until 1923, and the first Soviet version did not appear until 1926. We shall therefore deal here with the Class E 0–10–0s built between 1912 and 1923.

Just as the quest for higher performance on passenger duties had led in 1911 to the S Class 2–6–2 with its much larger boiler capacity, so the Russian railway authorities (with many years' experience of 0–8–0 and 2–8–0 locomotives) were studying the possibility of adopting the ten-coupled goods locomotive, as early as 1905 (see p. 32). Eventually the first locomotives of what was to become the largest single locomotive 'class group' ever known appeared in 1912, as the Class E 0–10–0. In August 1914, when several batches were already in service, the Ministry of Railways decided to concentrate on building Class E 0–10–0s, instead of Class Shch 2–8–0s, and by 1917 more than a thousand were in service. The assessment of the total quantity produced during this period is rendered very difficult by the use of different blocks of numbers for each builder, leaving large gaps in the sequence, but locomotives have been noted with numbers between E 37 and E 720, from E 1001 up to 1475, and from E 3001 to about 3275, plus a few odd numbers in the two-thousands. The 4000 and 5000 groups were left blank, but other batches began at 6001, 7001, 7601, 7801 and 8001 and were known collectively as the '1915 Type'. By the time the Revolution brought production to a virtual standstill at all the works concerned, the total of Class E locomotives is said to have reached one thousand one hundred and six.

After 1918, locomotive production in the newly-formed U.S.S.R. was almost at a standstill, fewer than one hundred units per year being produced; not until 1928 was the production figure for 1914 exceeded. In the meantime, the Soviet railways turned to foreign builders, and in 1920 placed orders in Sweden and Germany for no fewer than one thousand two hundred Class E 0–10–0s, the design adopted being that used by the Lugansk Works in 1917 for the E 7800 series. Five hundred were ordered from Nydqvist & Holm of Trollhättan, Sweden, of which the first fifteen were assembled at Lugansk and the rest shipped complete to the port of Riga, the only ice-free Baltic port where they could be unloaded direct on to 5 ft gauge tracks. These engines took the numbers E 4001 to 4500, with a sub-class letter sh ,for *Shvetsiya* (Sweden). According to Rakov, E 4016–4115 were subcontracted to Henschel.

The German order was spread among no fewer than nineteen different builders, in order to obtain quick delivery of the seven hundred machines involved, but all were alike and all took the sub-class letter g(r), for *Germaniya*. These locomotives were numbered from Eg 5000 to 5699; the first was delivered to Russia on 30 July 1921, and the last on 14 March 1923. The nineteen builders concerned were AEG, Borsig, Hanomag, Hartmann, Henschel, Hohenzollern, Esslingen, Humboldt, Jung, Karlsruhe, Krauss, Krupp, Linke-Hoffmann, Maffei, Orenstein & Koppel, Rhein-metall, Schwartzkopf, Wolff and Vulkan. At all events, it was an eloquent testimony to the productive capacity of the enormous German locomotive-building industry even in defeat.

With these additions, and some further construction in Russia, the number of Class E 0–10–0s of generally pre-Revolutionary design was brought up to somewhere between two thousand three hundred and fifty and two thousand eight hundred. It is unlikely that all have been scrapped yet, apart from war-losses, for many examples have been seen in all number-groups during the past ten years, though often serving such mundane purposes as station pilots.

The later Class E locomotives, to be dealt with in chapter 4, handle the majority of short-trip freight trains.

DIMENSIONS

Cylinders $25\frac{9}{16} \times 27\frac{9}{16}$ in. *Coupled wheels* 4 ft 4 in. dia. *Boiler pressure* 171 p.s.i. *Grate area* 45·2 ft². *Weight full* (*engine only*) 80 tons. *Max. axle load* 16·2 tons.

Class L (later **Lp**) (RUSSIAN Л [Лп]) *pl. 31*

The four-cylinder 'Pacifics' of Class L were designed in 1914 to work medium loads at maximum speeds of 65 to 75 m.p.h. Two sets of valve gear were fitted with rocking levers to operate the inside valves. The engines were numbered L 101 – 166 (numbers L 1 – 100 presumably being reserved for the Sormovo two-cylinder version cancelled owing to the war). In 1915–18 eighteen of them were constructed at Putilov as oil-burners for the Caucasian Railways. During 1923–6, forty-eight more were built for the principal fast trains on the Moscow–Leningrad line, where the earlier engines joined them in 1928–9. In the mid-1930s they were altered to coal-burners and went back to the South. Since the lines around Tiflis were then being electrified, most of them were put to work in the Ordzhonikidze region, on the North side of the mountains instead of the South. These engines proved to be less economical than the 2–6–2s. In 1947, when a new L class appeared, the classification was altered to Lp (L standing for Lopushinsky, the original designer, and p for Putilov).

DIMENSIONS

Cylinders (4) 18 × 25$\frac{9}{16}$ in. *Coupled wheels* 6 ft 0$\frac{1}{2}$ in. dia. *Boiler pressure* 171 p.s.i. *Grate area* 50 ft². *Weight full (engine only)* 102·7 tons. *Max. axle load* 16.2 tons.

Class Ye (RUSSIAN E) *pl. 37, 38*

The class designation of these 2–10–0 freight locomotives is the Russian letter which looks like a capital E but is actually 'Ye'. For this reason it has all too often been confused with the Class E (Э) 0–10–0.

The Ye 2–10–0 is an American design supplied to Russia during both World Wars, though here we are only concerned with those built up to 1918. In all, one thousand three hundred of them were ordered between 1915 and 1917, of which nine hundred were actually built up to the time delivery ceased for political reasons in July 1918. Another two hundred and forty-six were altered or completed to standard gauge and sold in the U.S.A. to the Erie, Seaboard Air Line and other railroads, and the remainder were cancelled.

These locomotives carry sub-class letters according to where they were built, the sub-class letters f (ф), s (c) and k denoting *Filadelfia* (Baldwin), Schenectady (Alco) and *Kanada* (Canadian Locomotive Company) respectively, though the locomotives from about 501 upward are of a slightly different version with sub-class letter n (H). The numbers of those delivered to Russia run from 1 to 800, 876 to 925 and 1126 to 1175, but since the total received is given as eight hundred and eighty-one (and not nine hundred) we assume one consignment of locomotives was lost at sea en route.

These locomotives, some of which still exist, have spent their entire working lives on the railways of Siberia and the Far East, for which they were designed; many of them at one time worked on the Chinese Eastern Railway, then of 5 ft gauge and under Russian control, and were presumably altered to standard gauge when the gauge of the railway was changed in 1935–6. Others remained in Russia, and an American traveller by the Trans-Siberian Railway in 1958 recalls his surprise and delight at stepping down from his train to stretch his legs and finding on the next track a Class Ye 2–10–0 bearing a 'Schenectady 1917' makers' plate. This particular locomotive was pumping water into the roof-tanks of his train, festooned with hoses.

DIMENSIONS

Cylinders 25 × 28 in. *Coupled wheels* 4 ft 4 in. dia. *Boiler pressure* 180 p.s.i. *Grate area* 64·5 ft². *Weight full* (*engine only*) 90 tons. *Max. axle load* 16·2 tons.

A 2–10–2 Tank engine version of the Ye class, weighing 125 tons, was built by the Skoda works in 1929. Six engines were supplied to the Chinese Eastern Railway and numbered Ь (soft sign) 4001–6.

Chapter 4

EARLY SOVIET-BUILT ENGINES

Class Su (RUSSIAN Cy) *pl. 34–36, 75*

We have seen how the Soviet railways, after the Revolution, inherited about nine hundred 2–6–2 passenger locomotives of Class S, built between 1911 and 1918. The superiority of these machines over all other passenger types was such that they were chosen as the future standard design for passenger work and an improved version, known as Class Su, was evolved by the Kolomna Works during 1925; the sub-class letter u again standing for *usilenny* (strengthened). Production was put in hand later in 1925, the first locomotive appearing early in the following year.

With this class the Russian railways adopted a new system of locomotive numbering known as the 'letter-and-cipher' system, though fortunately it was applied only to new locomotives and not to existing types. Its object was apparently to ensure that eventually every Russian locomotive would have a different serial number irrespective of its class letter, but to avoid 'solid' four-, five- and six-figure numbers the locomotives were to be numbered in groups of ninety-nine, divided by a stop from the parent hundreds. Since the largest existing class (the O Class 0–8–0) were numbered up into the low 9000s the first of the new locomotives became Su96·01, followed by Su96·02 up to 96·99, then 97·01 up to 97·99, and so on. The 'hundreds' number was left blank, perhaps so as not to cause confusion between, say, the existing 1912 locomotive S.96 and a new S96·00. Other blocks of numbers, such as 160·01 upwards, or 676·01 upwards, were used for other new classes, and presumably blocks of numbers were left vacant to receive existing classes when renumbered. But this never occurred, and the 'letter-and-cipher' system was itself replaced by a new system after 1931, although it has been retained for further construction of classes already numbered in this way.

About five hundred and fifty Class S locomotives were built to the 1926 design during the following four or five years, taking the numbers 96·01 to 99, 97·01 to 99, 98·01 to 99, 99·01 to 99, 100·01 to 99 and 101·01 to about 101·50; plenty of these have been noted at work during the past few years, including the second of them, Su96·02. In 1932 new construction was transferred to a new batch of numbers starting at Su200·01 and continued upwards through the series Su201 to 205 in 1933–35, Su206 to 215 in 1936–9 and Su216 to 218 in 1940–1, all from the Sormovo and Kolomna Works. Production ceased about half way through the Su218 series on account of the German invasion of Russia, by which time about two thousand four hundred locomotives of Class Su had appeared.

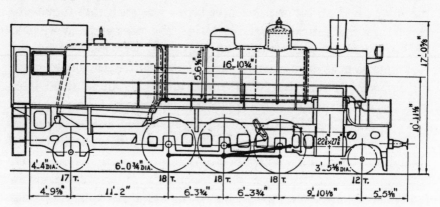

Class Su200

Some of the 1940 Kolomna batch of 2–6–2s, in the 216, 217 and 218 series, were turned out to an altered design known as Class Sum (the 'm' denoting 'modernised'). Production of the 2–6–2 was resumed after the war, the Sormovo Works producing a batch of Su locomotives numbered from Su250·01, beginning in August 1947, and continuing through the Su251, Su252 and Su253 series to somewhere in the Su254 batch, the highest number so far observed being Su254·10. It has been stated that some of the post-war locomotives were of the Sum type, but no such numbers have been reported. Production ceased in 1951, forty years after the first S Class 2–6–2 appeared in 1910, and bringing the all-time total of some three thousand seven hundred and fifty machines. Although outnumbered by several freight classes, this is by far the largest single passenger locomotive 'class group' in Russia, and rivalled in Europe only by the *Mädchen für alles* 38-class (Prussian P.8) 4–6–0s of the German railways, which also exceeded the three thousand mark.

The Su 2–6–2 handled the vast majority of steam-worked passenger trains in Russia, main-line, local and suburban; only on the most important trunk lines did one find anything larger at the head end. The number-batches do not seem to be allocated geographically, and locomotives of the same batch, with adjacent numbers, may be found hauling suburban trains at Leningrad and tourist expresses along the shores of the Black Sea, at least before the recent electrification. The 2–6–2s are the greyhounds of the Russian railways, and among their many notable performances was a test run from Moscow to Leningrad in November 1936, when a light train hauled by relays of Su 2–6–2s covered the 404 miles in only 6 hours 20 minutes, including engine changes.

DIMENSIONS

Officially the engines are classed Su, Su97, Su200 and Sum, the dimensions of Class Su97 being:

Cylinders $22\frac{5}{8} \times 27\frac{9}{16}$ in. *Coupled wheels* 6 ft $0\frac{3}{4}$ in. dia. *Boiler pressure* 185 p.s.i. *Grate area* 50·9 ft². *Weight full* (*engine only*) 84 tons. *Max. axle load* 18 tons.

Class Su200 are slightly heavier.

Class Sum weigh 90 tons with a max. axle load of 20 tons. They were built with fan draught and air pre-heaters.

Class M (RUSSIAN M) *pl. 32*

The only three-cylinder locomotives to have worked on the Soviet railways are the 4–8–0s of Class M. The design was originally in the hands of Professor A. S. Raevsky, who arranged the outside cranks at 90 deg. with the inside at 135 deg. to each, a setting which presumably indicated a Smith compound. However Raevsky died in 1924, and the usual 120-deg. crank setting was adopted by the Putilov Works where the engines were later built. Three sets of valve gear were used with a double return-crank on the left side.

The bogie was quite unique with wheels of 3 ft 5⅝ in diameter on the leading axle and 4 ft 4 in on the trailing.

The M Class, of which the first locomotive appeared in April 1927, were numbered from M 160·01 upwards, using the 1925 system of numbering. About eighty were built for heavy passenger service and they were put to work in the Urals. For some reason they rode so badly that they had to be run at reduced speed, and could only be used on short-distance freight trains or on engineers' trains, such as those carrying materials for track relaying. From 1934 onward they were rebuilt as two-cylinder engines, by removing the inside cylinders, increasing the pressure and re-setting the outside cranks at 90 deg., being re-classified Mr (reconstructed M). This rebuilding was evidently a success and the class was restored to passenger duties, their last reported use being on the Ozherelye–Pavelets–Michurinsk line prior to electrification.

DIMENSIONS

Cylinders (3) 21¼ × 27⁹⁄₁₆ in. *Coupled wheels* 5 ft 7¹¹⁄₁₆ in. dia. *Boiler pressure* 185 p.s.i. *Grate area* 64½ ft². *Weight full* (*engine only*) 99½ tons. *Max. axle load* 18.2 tons.

Class E (RUSSIAN Э) *pl. 28-30*

In the previous section, devoted to pre-Revolutionary locomotives types still in use, we mentioned the existence of between two thousand three hundred and fifty and two thousand eight hundred 0–10–0s of Class Э, built between 1912 and 1923. This would be a respectable total for a locomotive class anywhere, but a standardisation policy in a country as large as Russia can result in astronomical numbers of near-identical locomotives being built, and so it has been with the Class Э 0–10–0. Its wide range of use, coupled with the fact that freight duties and shunting account for 80 per cent of the Russian railways' engine-hours, have made the Class Э 0–10–0 the most common of all locomotive types on the Soviet railways.

Like the Class S 2–6–2, the Class Э 0–10–0 was chosen by the Soviet railways as the most suitable freight engine type for mass-production. During 1925, an improved version was designed and put into production at Briansk, appearing in 1926 with the classification Эu, the 'u' once again denoting *usilenny*, or 'more powerful'. Using the 1926 numbering system, these locomotives were probably numbered from Eu676·01 upwards, though the lowest number actually noted by travellers in Russia is 676·48. During the next seven years, from 1926 to 1933, they accounted for nearly three-fifths of the total Russian production of five thousand six hundred locomotives, the total of Eu 0–10–0s being about three thousand three hundred and fifty, in the number-series Eu676 to Eu680, Eu681 to Eu690, Eu691 to Eu700 and Eu701 to Eu709. Locomotives have been observed recently in all these series except Eu691 to 697, but there is little doubt that these also exist; possibly they are oil-burning engines used in the South, such as the Eu682 oil-burning series especially constructed for the Caucasian railways, burning locally-produced oil from the Baku fields. Five builders were concerned in turning out the pre-1933 Eu engines, namely Voroshilovgrad (ex-Lugansk), Kolomna, Sormovo, Kharkov and Briansk. A further batch of Eu machines was turned out a year later and numbered in the Eu712 series, probably bringing the total of these engines up to about three thousand four hundred and fifty.

So far we have accounted for between five thousand eight hundred and six thousand one hundred and fifty Class E 0–10–0s, but even greater totals were to follow. A much-improved version was evolved in 1931. The new version was known as Class Em 710xx, in batches of ninety-nine as before, up through the tens, twenties and thirties of the 700-range as far as the Em737 series, adding another two thousand seven hundred to the grand total of Class E 0–10–0s by about 1936, if all the number-series are complete, which is reported to be the case. During the war many Class Em locomotives were given a cylindrical additional water-tank on the tender to give increased range, for instance on military trains in areas where some of the regular sources of locomotive water may have been out of action, and many Em locomotives still carry the extra tank today. This temporary arrangement is liable to be mistaken for the cylindrical oil tanks to be seen on many tenders.

At the same time as the lighter Em sub-class was being produced another more powerful design, to be known as the Er (reconstructed E), was evolved by the Murom locomotive repair works, using locomotive Em723·12, which then became Er723·12 (Russian locomotives normally keeping their original serial num-

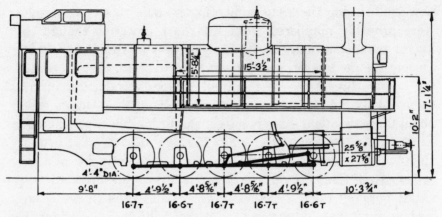

Class Er

ber on being rebuilt and reclassified). The 0–10–0 building programme at Briansk and Voroshilovgrad Works was turned over to this new design, and production continued through the Er738, 739, 740, 741, 742, 743, 744 and 745 series up to a highest reported number of Er 746·48, a presumed total of about eight hundred and fifty machines, most of which appeared in 1935 and 1936. By the outbreak of war the grand total of Class E 0–10–0s cn the Soviet railways must have been not far short of ten thousand; but still more were to follow.

It seems unlikely that any Class E 0–10–0s were built during the years immediately preceding 1941, but in 1944 some of Class Er were rebuilt at Kolomna with boilers taken from the latest version of the Class Su 2–6–2s. This rebuild also differed in having a single dome and sandbox casing instead of three separate structures, and had the distinctive clerestory cab as on the more modern designs. With Su boilers the pressure is 185 lb and the grate area 50·9 ft², the engines being classed Esu.

At the end of the war the Russian railways found themselves in desperate need of additional freight locomotives to make good the ravages of war and obsolescence, and while their own factories concentrated on 2–10–0 locomotives, large orders for Class Er 0–10–0s were placed in the satellite states of Eastern Europe. These engines also had the combined dome and sandbox casings. The total quantity supplied by each country, and the numbering of the respective batches, is not known for certain, but locomotives have been noted with builders' plates of Resita (Roumania) in

48

series E762 and E767, of Mavag (Budapest) in series E768, E774, E775, E776, E797, E798 and E799, of Ceskomoravska-Kolben-Danek in series E770 and E772, and of Polish builders in series E785 and E786. Other locomotives of the same Class have been noted with numbers in the E760, E761, E766, E788, E789, E790 and E791 series, and the total Hungarian production of these machines has been given in a trade journal as one thousand five hundred, plus a few built for the Hungarian railways and used for shunting on broad-gauge tracks at the frontier station with Russia. If all the number-series from E760 to E799 are complete the total would be another three thousand five hundred, but if the apparent gaps between certain series are correct, the total imported since 1946 is nearer two thousand one hundred. The absence of exact figures is the more regrettable since the post-war Class E 0–10–0s bring the grand total for this class-group up to somewhere between twelve thousand and thirteen thousand five hundred, in either case well in excess of what is often claimed to be the largest locomotive class-group in the world, the German 2–10–0s of Classes 50, 50 UK, 42 and 52, which are said to have reached a total of ten thousand six hundred and fifty.

With such a total it goes without saying that the Class E 0–10–0 was the most common sight on Russian railways, and apart from war losses the entire class lasted until c. 1960, several original machines of 1912–13 having been noted in use during 1959. It is a sobering thought that *one single class* of Russian locomotive was barely less than the entire steam locomotive stock of British railways.

DIMENSIONS: Class Eu

Cylinders $25\frac{9}{16} \times 27\frac{9}{16}$ in. *Coupled wheels* 4 ft 4 in. dia. *Boiler pressure* 171 p.s.i. *Grate area* 48 ft². *Weight full (engine only)* 83·2 tons. *Max. axle load* 16·7 tons.

Class Em: as above, but boiler pressure 199 p.s.i.; weight 84·9 tons and max. axle load, 17 tons.

Class Er: as Em, with grate area increased to 54·7 ft², weight increased to 87·2 tons and max. axle load increased to 17½ tons.

Chapter 5

THE BIG ENGINE PERIOD

To the student of the locomotive the most fascinating of all periods in the development of Russian railway motive power was that in which the Soviet railways set out to transform their system from a railway on the European model to one comparable in many ways with those of North America, a transformation now almost complete. It has been said that the Russian railways before 1914 combined the disadvantages of both the European and American systems (short trains and low-capacity wagons coupled with low line capacity), whereas the system today operates American-length trains with European frequency. Although the average Russian freight train is still not quite the equal of its American counterpart, the visitor will certainly recognise the validity of this comparison on seeing the trains of long bogie wagons, the virtual absence of four-wheel main-line goods stock, the use of automatic couplings and the size of the modern locomotives. As in other fields such as steel production and automobile engineering, the new Soviet State did not allow ideological differences to prevent its adopting ideas from American technology and this development was largely a product of the first Five-Year Plan, of 1928–32.

Prior to this period, the size of the locomotives in use was limited to that permitted by an axle load of 16–17 tons, few lines being able to accommodate anything above this figure. Since then the Russian railways have progressively upgraded their lines by using heavier rail, and a figure of 22 tons per axle is now common on main lines, while the latest class of electric locomotive to be produced in quantity has an axle load of 23 tons. This development has taken place over a period of some thirty years, and in two main stages, the initial aim in the 1931–7 period being a network of trunk lines with a standard axle-loading of 20 metric tons, worked by freight locomotives capable of hauling trains of from 2500 to 3000 tons.

Class T (RUSSIAN T)

In the early stages it would appear that the higher figure of 23 tons per axle was already contemplated as the new standard, for in 1930 the Soviet railways after sending over a study group of engineers, ordered ten locomotives in America with this axle load and tender boosters. The locomotives were shipped to Leningrad in the autumn of 1931; five were 2–10–4s (Ta 10000–4) built by the American Locomotive Company and five were 2–10–2s (Tb 10005–9) by Baldwin. Both were given class letter T, with sub-class a for the Alco locomotives and b for the Baldwins, and both classes were fitted with American-type heavy-duty automatic couplings which were realised by the Soviet railways to be essential for working trains of the tonnage envisaged. Since, however, neither the track nor the existing couplings of the freight stock were such as to permit the regular operation of such trains at that period, it seems unlikely that the American engines saw much service for the first year or two. Twenty-five years were to elapse before the change to automatic couplings (begun in 1932) was completed, while the adoption of a general 23-ton axle load for trunk lines has still not been achieved today. However, after an initial sojourn in the Dnepropetrovsk region, scope was found for the American engines on short hauls with specialised iron-ore trains in the Stalinsk (Kuznetsk) district of Siberia, presumably over a route laid or relaid to the heavier standard and with stock equipped with automatic couplers. It is here that the ten American engines are thought to have spent almost the whole of their working lives.

No. AA 20-1 *pl. 41*

Although steel production increased rapidly under the first and second Five-Year Plans (1929–32 and 1933–7), the adoption of a 23-ton axle load as the main-line standard would have required an enormous tonnage of new and heavier rail, and it appears that (perhaps because of the many conflicting demands for steel) the railways were obliged to adopt an interim main-line standard of 20 tons per axle. Towards the end of 1931 the Moscow Institute of Transport Engineers was given the task of establishing the maximum freight locomotive dimensions and performance attainable with the 20-ton axle load (the new rail weight being 78 lb per yard), and produced a design for a seven-coupled locomotive with the wheel arrangement 2–14–4. This was later modified to 4–14–4, and a prototype locomotive was constructed at the Voroshilovgrad Works during 1934. It was given the class designation AA, in honour of Andrei Andreyev, its sponsor, and numbered AA 20–1, the 20 denoting the axle-load. Considerable opposition to the project had been expressed at a previous Party Session by the more practical members who had pressed for more 2–10–2s in its place.

Although intended, according to the press statements, for the Moscow–Donbass coal traffic, this mammoth locomotive does not appear to have performed any revenue service whatever, though it successfully made a 'press trip' to Moscow in January 1935, and achieved a great deal of publicity as the largest non-articulated locomotive in Europe and the locomotive with the largest number of coupled axles in the world. For many years its subsequent history was unknown, and only recently have Russian technical publications admitted that the locomotive was an operating failure in that it caused the track to spread, damaged the points and was very prone to derailment. The design was not repeated, and the prototype locomotive spent the rest of its life in store; the precise date of its eventual scrapping is unknown. Some may perhaps regret that this machine was not preserved as a museum-piece, but practical Russian railwaymen were probably heartily glad to see the last of it.

DIMENSIONS

Cylinders 29⅛ × 31⅞ in. *Coupled wheels* 5 ft 3 in. dia. *Boiler pressure* 242 p.s.i. *Grate area* 129 ft². *Weight full (engine only)* 208 tons. *Max. axle load* 20 tons.

Beyer-Garratt Ya-01 (RUSSIAN Я-01) *pl. 40*

Although the maximum-size rigid wheel base locomotive was regarded with some scepticism outside the U.S.S.R. (and probably inside too), the Russian railways were well aware of the advantages of articulated locomotives. Considerable use had been made in the past of Fairlie and Mallet engines, and in 1932 a trial Beyer-Garratt locomotive was obtained from Messrs Beyer Peacock & Co, of Manchester, with the wheel arrangement 4–8–2 + 2–8–4. This was required to meet the same specification of hauling a 2,500-ton train with an axle load not exceeding 20 tons. The resulting locomotive weighed 266 tons and was the largest steam locomotive to have been built in Europe. It was given the number Ya–01 (the letter Ya (Я) being one of the few not currently occupied by a locomotive class) and after being shipped to Leningrad entered service in 1933 on the Sverdlovsk–Chelyabinsk line of the South Urals railway, where it underwent extensive trials.

According to Mr P. E. Garbutt, the maintenance requirements of this locomotive did not accord with Russian operating conditions, and it was eventually dismantled in 1937. A model of it can be seen, together with several others, at the Leningrad Railway Museum.

DIMENSIONS
Cylinders (4) $22\frac{7}{16} \times 29\frac{1}{8}$ in. *Coupled wheels* 4 ft 11 in. dia. *Boiler pressure* 220 p.s.i. *Grate area* 86 ft². *Weight full* 266 tons. *Max. axle load* 20 tons.

Class FD (RUSSIAN ФД) *pl. 42–4, 70*

With the decision to adopt a 20-ton axle load as the new standard, the Soviet railways drew up in a remarkably short time, early in 1931, a design for a freight locomotive based broadly on the prototype American designs then on order, but limited to an adhesive weight of 100 tons, giving 20 tons on each coupled axle. The result was the Felix Dzherzhinsky 2–10–2, the first of several locomotive classes to be named after political notabilities. The first locomotive was completed at the Voroshilovgrad Works on 6 November 1931, the building time being only 170 days. Bar frames, mechanical stoker and a large boiler with steel firebox and combustion chamber were amongst the American features introduced; cow-catchers and clerestory cab roofs were provided for the first time on a new class. The twelve-wheel tenders holding 22 tons of coal and 10,000 gallons of water were far larger than earlier classes. In future all boilers with a grate area of over 64 ft² were to be provided with mechanical stokers.

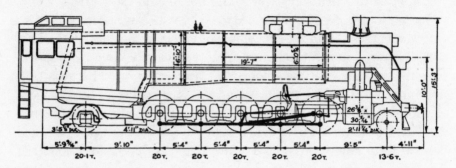

Class FD20

The 'big engine' policy marked a complete break with the earlier practice of building locomotives which could work over virtually any section of the U.S.S.R. railway system; in future, operating staffs would have to relate the make-up and motive power of any train to the axle load permitted on the lines to be traversed. To provide a simple and foolproof reminder of the axle load of a locomotive it was decided to amplify the numbering system for types in excess of the standard-ton figure by including it in the class designation. The first 'Felix Dzherzhinsky' locomotive therefore received the number FD20·01, and the 4–14–4 the number AA20–1, the 20 in each case representing the axle load (in metric tons).

The FD locomotive proved very satisfactory and was adopted in 1933 as the standard design for freight service on upgraded trunk lines. Production began at the Voroshilovgrad Works with locomotive FD20–02 in 1933, and continued at about four hundred per year until the German invasion of the Ukraine, by which time just over three thousand two hundred locomotives of this class had been turned out; the highest serial number reported by travellers is 3,219. The final two hundred and sixty or so locomotives were built to a slightly heavier design, the FD21, for service on certain lines which could now permit an axle-loading of 21 tons.

During the war large numbers of FD locomotives were success-fully evacuated from European Russia in the face of the German advance, but were too heavy for use on the lightly-laid lines behind the front, which had suddenly been thrust into strategic promin-ence. During 1943 and 1944, a total of eighty-five FD locomo-tives were therefore temporarily rebuilt as 2–10–4s with an axle load of only 18 tons (Class FD18), the first being FD18·598. With the turn of the tide this rebuilding ceased, and the locomo-tives concerned later reverted to their original wheel arrangement and classification. Recent modifications include heightened chim-neys and smoke deflectors on many of them.

No further FD locomotives have been built since the war, but many of them were working until recently on the lines south of Moscow, particularly in the Ukraine and the Donbass. With the spread of electrification to the most heavily-utilised lines the sphere of use for the FD locomotive contracted, and in 1958 several hundred of the class were sold to China, where they were converted to standard gauge and termed the 'Friendship' class (*pl.* 70). Those remaining in the U.S.S.R. are thought to have been withdrawn about four years ago.

DIMENSIONS

Cylinders 26⅜ × 30⁵⁄₁₆ in. *Coupled wheels* 4 ft 11 in. dia. *Boiler pressure* 213 p.s.i. *Grate area* 75¾ ft². *Weight full (engine only)* 135 tons. *Max. axle load* 20 tons.

Class IS (RUSSIAN ИС) *pl. 45, 46*

Although the Russian railways have always placed far greater importance on freight than on passenger traffic, the up-grading of main lines to 'trunk lines' with a 20-ton axle load also held out promise of greatly increased productivity in passenger traffic, by running heavier trains to the same schedules. To realise these possibilities it was necessary to construct a passenger equivalent of the FD2–10–2, and this design emerged a year later.

The new locomotive was a 2–8–4, with many parts (including the boiler) interchangeable with the 2–10–2. It was named in honour of Joseph Stalin, taking the number IS20·1, with the name repeated in a half-circle at the top of the smokebox. This first locomotive was completed by the Kolomna Works in October

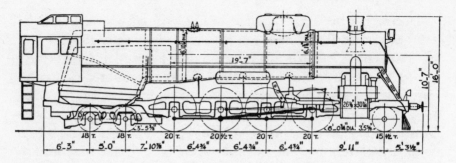

Class IS

1932, and was followed a year later by the slightly different
IS20·2, which is at present in service at Kiev. Four more locomotives appeared in 1934–5, and after a good part of the leeway
in freight motive power had been made good, the Voroshilovgrad
Works in 1937 began the series-production of 2–8–4s, one of the
first (IS20·16) being turned out with streamlining. Production
continued until 1941, the total being some six hundred and forty
locomotives of Class IS20, followed by ten heavier machines with
the classification IS21, one example reported being IS21·646.
Production of this type ceased in 1941, the equivalent post-war
type being a new 4–8–4, and in 1962 the Joseph Stalin engines
were renamed FDp (Felix Dzherzhinsky, Passenger). They
worked on almost all of the non-electrified trunk lines to the south
and east of Moscow, taking over from electric locomotives at the
limits of the Moscow area electrification. One of the 2–8–4s, in
light blue livery, together with an FD2–10–2, was exhibited at
the Paris Exhibition of 1937, having been shipped via Dunkerque.

DIMENSIONS
Cylinders 26⅜ × 30‑5/16 in. *Coupled wheels* 6 ft 0¾ in. dia. *Boiler
pressure* 213 p.s.i. *Grate area* 75¾ ft². *Weight full (engine only)* 134
tons. *Max. axle load* 20·4 tons.

Class SO (RUSSIAN CO) *pl. 48–50, 72*

The 'big engine' policy did not remove the necessity of re-
placing many old locomotives working lightly-laid lines, nor of
producing lighter machines for the many new lines under construction, only a few of which were of trunk line status. We have
seen in the previous chapter how production of the Class E 0–10–0

and Class Su 2–6–2 continued throughout the 1930s, though the rate of production of the 0–10–0 declined appreciably after about 1935, being replaced by a new 2–10–0 design.

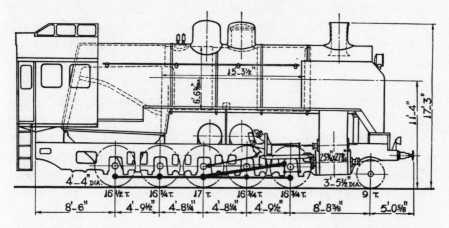

Class SO17

This light axle load 2–10–0, the first of which appeared in 1934, was developed from the Em 0–10–0 and named after Sergo Ordzhonikidze, the first locomotive taking the number SO17·1. Production began in 1935, and so far as is known, about one thousand nine hundred locomotives had appeared by 1941, including about one thousand two hundred with condensing tenders for use in waterless and bad-water regions; these (classed SO19) are dealt with in chapter 10. The main centres of production were the Briansk, Kharkov and Voroshilovgrad Works, but the SO Class was chosen for the initial programme of two new locomotive-building works set up in Siberia: the Ulan-Ude Works in 1938 and the Krasnoyarsk Works in 1943. The latter was set up with the equipment evacuated from Voroshilovgrad at the time of the German invasion of the Ukraine.

The existence of these works enabled production of the SO Class 2–10–0 to continue during the war, though not in large numbers. The Ulan-Ude design differed slightly from the pre-war locomotives, and took 'u' as sub-class letter, thus becoming SO17u Class.

When production was started again at the Voroshilovgrad Works in 1945 the locomotives produced were initially of a heavier version, the SO18, of which some examples from 1939–40 already existed. Relatively few of these machines were built,

57

however, and from about SO17·2301 upwards, production reverted to the SO17 design, the full resources of Voroshilovgrad being also engaged in this programme for the next three years. During this period about one thousand eight hundred Class SO 2–10–0s were built, bringing the numbers into the four-thousands. Several hundred further examples have been added since 1949, the highest numbers so far observed being SO17·4667 (which probably appeared around 1954) and, after a large gap, SO17·6011. The last would seem to indicate another group, numbered SO17·6001 upwards.

There are many gaps in the number sequence of SO class 2–10–0s reported by travellers in Russia, for instance between 3,500 and 3,999, but it is possible that locomotives of these numbers were built at the two Siberian production centres for service in their own districts. If the number-series are complete (except the 5xxx), as is probably the case, the total number of SO Class 2–10–0s, including condensing locomotives, is therefore about five thousand.

DIMENSIONS Class SO18

Cylinders 25$\frac{9}{16}$ × 27$\frac{9}{16}$ in. *Coupled wheels* 4 ft 4 in. dia. *Boiler pressure* 199 p.s.i. *Grate area* 64$\frac{1}{2}$ ft². *Weight full (engine only)* 97 tons. *Max. axle load* 17$\frac{1}{2}$ tons.

Class 2-3-2 *pl. 47*

In general the Russian railways concentrate on building very large numbers of locomotives to a few standard designs, rather than evolving special types for special jobs. An exception to this rule was however made for Russia's crack train, the 'Red Arrow' (*Krasnaya Strela*) on the overnight service between Moscow and Leningrad. The 404-mile main line between the two principal cities of the Union was selected for equipment with new rail permitting an axle-loading of 21 tons and, in November 1937, the Kolomna Works produced the first of an order for ten streamlined 4–6–4 locomotives for this duty. It was intended to work the 'Red Arrow' completely with this type of locomotive; with two engine changes en route (at Kalinin and Bologoye), six locomotives would be needed daily to maintain the service. When all were delivered it was hoped to cut the ten-hour schedule for the

404 miles to one of eight hours, but the war intervened and this aim was never realised with steam traction.

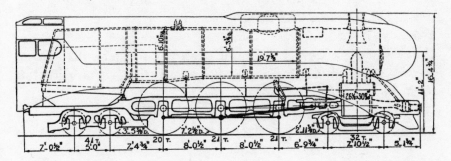

Engine 2–3–2 No. 3

The prototype was numbered 2–3–2 No.1, without any class letter and when on trial on the October Railway near Kalinin on 29 June 1938, reached a speed of 106 m.p.h., which still stands as the Russian official speed record for steam traction. This figure was the more creditable for being attained on a level road, with no assistance from falling gradients.

Meanwhile the second engine, 2–3–2 No. 2, had appeared from Kolomna in May, with a different superheater and tube arrangement, whilst a third had already emerged from Voroshilovgrad in April as No. 6998 (its Works' number). This latter was an alternative design, with larger coupled wheels, incorporating as many parts of the IS and FD Classes as possible. It seems probable that further construction was halted until the relative merits of these three trial engines could be established, and that war intervened, preventing, as Rakov states, continuation of the project. Confirmation comes from another post-war Russian book which mentions three engines only as K1, K2 and V (Kolomna 1 and 2, and Voroshilovgrad).

Only two of these engines (2–3–2 No. 2 and 2–3–2 No. 3) have been seen at work in recent years. The latter was seen by one of the authors in July 1957, at Kalinin, ready to haul the 'Red Arrow' on the last stage of its journey into Moscow (2–3–2 No. 3 being No. 6998 renumbered). A year after the visit just mentioned the 'Red Arrow' was taken over by diesel locomotives, and no further reports of the 4–6–4s at work have come in.

DIMENSIONS: 2–3–2 Nos 1 and 2

Cylinders 22$\frac{13}{16}$ × 27$\frac{9}{16}$ in. *Coupled wheels* 6 ft 6$\frac{11}{16}$ in. dia. *Boiler pressure* 213 p.s.i. *Grate area* 70 ft². *Weight full* (*engine only*) 123$\frac{1}{2}$ tons. *Max. axle load* 20·9 tons.

2–3–2 No 3.

Cylinders 26$\frac{3}{8}$ × 30$\frac{5}{16}$ in. *Coupled wheels* 7 ft 2$\frac{1}{2}$ in. dia. *Boiler pressure* 213 p.s.i. *Grate area* 75$\frac{3}{4}$ ft². *Weight full* (*engine only*) 138 tons. *Max. axle load* 21·3 tons.

Class **LK** (RUSSIAN ЛК)

This locomotive, if it ever existed, is one of the enigmas of the Russian railway scene. It was intended as a heavy-duty passenger 2–8–4 to succeed the IS Class as and when a sufficient mileage of lines had been upgraded to permit a 23-ton axle-load, the original design being worked out at Voroshilovgrad. The project was later transferred to Kolomna, and Baron Vuillet, writing in *Chemins de Fer* for June 1947, states that a prototype locomotive was completed in February 1941, and carried out extensive tests in April of that year. The letters LK, by which the class was to be known, were the initials of Mr Lazar Kaganovitch, Commissar of Transport and Heavy Industry.

More recent sources, however, suggest that although the design was undoubtedly prepared and published, no locomotive of this type was ever built. Certainly no mention of it appears in Rakov's or other recent Russian works, and it may well be that the programme of re-equipping main lines with heavier rail was not sufficiently far advanced to justify construction of this type and that the project, deferred owing to the German invasion, was never revived.

Chapter 6

WAR-TIME ACQUISITIONS

The pride of the Russian railways in their locomotives, particularly in those new designs marking a notable step forward, has had the result that many of the classes, such as the FD and the IS, are quite familiar to locomotive students of other countries through being mentioned in Russian publicity material. There is however another category of Russian steam locomotive about which far less has been published, since these machines rarely if ever appear in such literature; we refer to the reparations locomotives captured from the Germans or taken over with new territory.

The Russian railways divided their wartime-acquired locomotives into the following three groups:

1. Locomotives taken over with the absorption of Latvia, Lithuania, Estonia and parts of Poland into the Soviet Union (1939–40).

2. Locomotives supplied by the American Government under Lease-Lend to make good Russia's wartime loss of locomotive production.

3. Locomotives captured in war from the attacking powers or obtained as reparations after the war from the same countries, principally Germany, Austria, Hungary and Roumania.

Of these, the first group of locomotives kept their original classification and number, and stayed in their original territories, whereas the last group were mostly reclassified and used wherever suitable work was to be found for them. Both groups had of course been converted to the Russian 5 ft gauge (1524 mm), except for a few standard gauge locomotives retained for shunting at the frontier stations. Report has it that there is also one line near the Hungarian border where, on account of a tunnel of restricted dimensions, the standard gauge has been retained, with a small stock of standard-gauge locomotives, carriages and wagons.

Polish locomotives taken over in 1939

In November 1939, the Russians took over the railways in what had been the easternmost provinces of Poland and converted them and their rolling stock to the broad gauge. The locomotives absorbed were a very mixed collection consisting of new Polish types, ex-Prussian machines and a few ex-Austrian types: 24 tender- and 9 tank-engine designs in all. After being over-run by the German Army in 1941, these lines and their rolling stock again came into Russian hands in 1944–5, but many of the older loco-motives taken over have since been retired and replaced by Russian types or ex-German reparations machines. The more modern Polish types are however present in force, and at the former Polish town of Lvov is a stud of about twenty passenger 2–8–2s of Class Pt31. These have retained their Polish numbers, with their class, transcribed into Russian. Examples of this class seen there during 1959 included Pt 31·9, 10, 14, 18, 28, 42, 61, 79 and 84. The 31 denotes the year in which the class of locomotive first appeared.

Two modern Polish freight types taken over are the 2–10–0s of Classes Ty23 and Ty37 (1923 and 1937 respectively), *pl.53*. In these cases the class designation could not be repeated exactly in Russian as the language has no letter representing the consonant 'y'; instead, the Russian equivalent adopted was Tu, which appears in Cyrillic as Ty, thus leaving the actual numbering on the locomo-tive unchanged! During the German advance, some of the 2–10–0s of Class Ty23 were successfully evacuated, and were put to work on the Turksib Railway in Asia, but appear to have since returned to their own depots near the Polish frontier, where several were seen at work during 1959.

Other modern Polish classes of which a few examples worked in Russia are the 4–6–0 Class Ok22, the 4–8–0 of Class Os24 and the 2–10–2 tank of Class Okz32. The latter engines were probably the only really large tank engines to be found in the Soviet Union. Photographs suggest that the standard gauge locomotives presented to Albania by Russia in 1946–7 included some former Polish tank engines.

Locomotives of the Baltic States

In 1940, the Baltic States of Estonia, Latvia and Lithuania were re-absorbed into Russia, bringing with them a total of about seven hundred locomotives, about a quarter of them narrow-gauge. Even the broad- and standard-gauge types were of a wonderful diversity and it is not surprising that most were withdrawn after 1945 and replaced mostly by ex-German machines.

In Estonia, the main-line railways were already of Russian broad gauge and the locomotive stock consisted mainly of Russian types built before 1918 and taken over when Estonia became independent after the first World War. Thus the standard goods locomotive in Estonia was the Russian O Class 0–8–0, and many passenger trains were hauled by N Class 2–6–0s. These were easily reabsorbed into their parent classes, but there were also some ex-Russian 0–6–0s of such antiquity that the equivalent class in Russia had by then disappeared; 0–6–0 locomotives dating back to the 1860s were by no means rare. New construction during the country's period of independence had consisted mainly of 2–4–2 and 2–6–2 tank engines,

In Latvia, most of the railway mileage was also of Russian gauge and similarly worked by ex-Russian types, including O Class 0–8–0s, N Class 2–6–0s, B Class 4–6–0s and also some S Class 2–6–2s, to which had been added several new classes, mainly 2–4–2 and 2–6–2 tank engines built in Germany or Finland and supplied with duplicate wheelsets that enabled them to be used on either broad or standard gauge. There were also some unusual modern 2–2–2 Tanks built locally at Riga from parts supplied by Henschel. These were probably the last single-driver engines to be built. On the lines to the South, which were of standard gauge, the locomotives were mainly of pre-1918 designs and only the larger ones were converted to broad gauge, the remainder being scrapped. In 1960, Latvia presented the spectacle of a Russian railway division worked almost entirely by ex-

German engines, the only Russian type in general use being the S Class 2–6–2 (of both Russian and ex-Latvian origin), while almost every freight train is headed by an ex-Reichsbahn 2–10–0; German locomotives also perform almost all shunting duties.

The Lithuanian railways were of standard gauge and worked mainly with ex-Prussian locomotive types obtained as reparations after 1918, but there were also some ex-Russian 0–8–0s of Class O (converted to standard gauge) and some new engines including a class of 2–4–4 tanks. These, and the best of the ex-German types, were changed to Russian gauge, but today, as in Latvia, the predominant steam locomotive is the ex-Reichsbahn wartime 2–10–0.

Class Sh,a (RUSSIAN Шa) *pl. 39*

Under the American Government's Lease-Lend programme a large number of locomotives was supplied to Russia between 1943 and 1946, (the last few in 1947). The first to be delivered, in 1943, were two hundred 2–8–0s of the standard American Army type also used in Europe and Korea, and based on the similar design used by the American Army in France during the first war. Of the two hundred, ninety were built by Baldwin and one hundred and ten by the American Locomotive Company.

These locomotives were allotted U.S. Army Transportation Corps numbers, but on being diverted to Russia were renumbered as Russian Class Sh (Ш) with numbers from 1 to 200. From this, it may be assumed that the survivors of the previous Sh Class (a Tsarist 2–8–0 design, a predecessor of the Shch Class described in chapter 3) had by this time disappeared, but to avoid any possible confusion the American locomotives were given a sub-class letter a (for 'American'). They were not specifically designed for Russian needs, but were later modified with the usual Russian weatherproofed cab. In 1947 the whole class was concentrated in the Leningrad-Tallinn area, where many of them were seen at work between 1956 and 1960. Although designed as freight locomotives, they are classed by the Russian railway as light-duty machines; some of those observed were hauling suburban trains or empty passenger stock at Leningrad terminal stations, and working in the docks.

Class Ye (RUSSIAN E) *pl. 37, 38*

While the two hundred U.S. Army 2–8–0s were being prepared for shipment to Russia in 1943, a Russian technical mission in the U.S.A. negotiated the supply under Lease-Lend of a much larger number of steam locomotives, to be built especially for Russian conditions. To save time, it was decided to adopt the same design of 2–10–0 that was supplied to Russia between 1915 and 1918, and these also took the class letter Ye, with the addition of a sub-class letter a. They were numbered from Ye,a2001 upwards, and in all two thousand one hundred and twenty locomotives were supplied between 1944 and 1947, numbered from 2001 to 4000 and from 4141 to 4260. Of these, one thousand one hundred and twenty-nine were built by Baldwin and nine hundred and ninety-one by Alco. The last twenty to be built were diverted to Finland.

These locomotives were transported across America on flatcars and shipped from Portland (Oregon) to Vladivostok in Russian vessels, since Russia was not at war with Japan. Each vessel could take eighteen locomotives. On arrival in the U.S.S.R. they were put to work on the Far Eastern lines together with their first-war classmates, proving very useful in hauling the large quantities of other Lease-Lend goods then being supplied to Russia. They were also used on the central section of the Trans-Siberian Railway and its principal branches, and a few were still in use as station pilots in 1970.

The 2–8–0 and 2–10–0 designs between them made a total of two thousand three hundred and twenty main-line steam locomotives supplied to Russia under Lease-Lend. In addition, America supplied one hundred diesel locomotives, of which twelve were lost at sea and the others delivered by the Trans-Iranian route, running on standard-gauge bogies from the Persian Gulf to the Caspian. There were also forty-two broad-gauge 0–6–0 tank engines and forty-six narrow-gauge engines, bringing the final Lease-Lend total to two thousand four hundred and eight.

Roumanian Locomotives

In 1940, the Roumanian province of Bessarabia was ceded to Russia and its railways became the Kishinev division of the

U.S.S.R. railways, the lines and the ex-Roumanian locomotives being converted to the Russian gauge. As in the case of the Baltic States, the locomotives kept their former numbers. In 1941, however, Roumania joined Germany in attacking the Soviet Union, taking over a large slice of Russian territory in addition to Bessarabia, and renumbered many captured Russian locomotives into C.F.R. (Roumanian State Railways) numbering, so that it was possible to see Russian locomotives lettered in Latin instead of Cyrillic script.

Nevertheless, a few ex-Roumanian locomotives from the Kishinev district were evacuated with the retreating Russian Army, and spent the war working as far away as Tashkent. With Roumania's declaration of war on the Soviet Union these locomotives were thenceforward considered as captured enemy property, and became the forerunners of a huge group of locomotives classed as *Trofiya* ('War-booty').

A 'War-booty' locomotive, whether captured in war or obtained afterwards as reparations, retains its original serial number but receives a new class designation prefixed by the letter T, for *Trofiya*. The second letter is that of the most nearly equivalent Russian class; for example, some of the captured Roumanian locomotives were of the German-built 2–8–0 Class 140, generally similar to the Prussian G 8². Considered as approximately equivalent to the Russian O Class 0–8–0 in range of duties, they were thus classed TO. Many more of these machines were taken over in 1944–5, and about twenty have been noted by travellers, the numbers ranging between TO402 and TO526. Since 'War-booty' locomotives retain their former numbers, these do not form a complete series and the numbers are not a true guide to the total number in the class.

Another Roumanian class was the 0–10–0 Class 50, generally similar to the Prussian G 10. In this case the equivalent Russian class was considered to be the Ye 2–10–0 and the locomotives were therefore reclassified as TYe, though one cannot help wondering whether, in view of the wheel arrangement, it should not have been TE. The third Roumanian class concerned was the 230 Class 4–6–0, based on the Prussian P 8, but in this case, although similar to the Russian K Class, the locomotives appear to have kept their Roumanian classification. None of them has been noted by travellers in Russia, and it may be that only some half-dozen machines in this class were acquired.

Class TE (RUSSIAN T9)

As the German armies pushed into Russia they needed large numbers of locomotives to maintain their supply lines, which were rapidly converted by German Army engineers to standard gauge. This need was filled for the most part by large numbers of austerity 2–10–0s of the Deutsche Reichsbahn Class 52, aided by others of Classes 50, 50 UK and 42. More than six thousand 2–10–0s of Class 52 were built and, together with the 'peacetime' and 'semi-austerity' versions (50 and 50UK) and the heavier Class 42, formed what was probably at that time the most numerous steam locomotive 'class group' in the world. Only with the construction in 1946–50 of further Russian E Class 0–10–0s (mentioned in chapter 4), was this distinction finally and indisputably regained by the Soviet Union.

Of the six thousand or so 52 Class 2–10–0s, it seems likely that rather more than one-third were built specifically for service in Russia, including some with ten-wheeled condensing tenders whose length prevented their being used in Germany itself. (Those that returned to Western Germany have now been scrapped and the tender underframes used for new ten-wheeled iron-ore wagons.) Hundreds of 52 Class 2–10–0s were captured by the Russian Army during the German retreat, and there is poetic justice in the fact that they stayed at work on the lines for which they were designed, though under Russian instead of German auspices.

The 52 Class was allotted the Russian classification TE, as being roughly equivalent in performance to the E Class 0–10–0. The serial number of the locomotive was retained, thus German 52,1497 became Russian TE1497, about two hundred actual numbers having been noted by recent travellers, ranging from TE004 through all the various series up to TE 7791. There is no knowing exactly how many of these locomotives the Russian railways owned, but the figure is thought to be somewhere between one thousand two hundred and fifty and two thousand. Being designed for Russian service, with fully-enclosed cabs, they were quite popular with Russian crews. They were the first sight encountered by the traveller entering Russia by rail from Poland, Czechoslovakia or Roumania, since a few had been kept as standard gauge machines for shunting at the gauge-conversion yards where through trains are jacked up and their bogies changed for the different gauge. In recent years many have been sold to Bulgaria, Czechoslovakia and Hungary.

Included in the TE Class are two further batches of German or German-type 2–10–0s. In addition to the 52 Class, the Soviet railways acquired a number of the semi-austerity 50UK loco-motives, recognisable by the juxtaposition of single-window cabs and straight-sided instead of semi-cylindrical ('Wannen') tenders. These locomotives have been grouped into a separate series start-ing at TE8001 and consisting probably of less than one hundred examples. A second group consists of a few 52 Class locomotives built in Roumania for the Roumanian State Railways as Class 150^{10}, which are numbered from TE9101 upwards; their total is probably less than two dozen.

Unlike the 52 Class with its 15-ton axle load and wide avail-ability, the heavier wartime 42 Class German 2–10–0 with an 18-ton axle load was generally employed nearer home rather than on hastily restored lines near the Front. Nevertheless, one hundred and fifty to two hundred of these locomotives fell into Russian hands, and when regauged were given the classification TL, the Russian class equivalent in power output being the L Class 2–10–0 described in chapter 7.

Other German Classes

Although the Reichsbahn 2–10–0s form by far the largest group of German locomotives acquired by Russia, small numbers of at least ten other German classes were also taken over between 1943 and 1945. Some of these were captured on the Russian front, but others formed the stock of the Königsberg division of the Reichsbahn, in that part of East Prussia now in the Soviet Union. Reports from travellers to this district are few, but it would seem that regauged German locomotives still perform a good proportion of the local work.

Prominent among the Königsberg (now Kaliningrad) stud were a few 'Pacifics' of Class 03, and these were given the Russian class designation TS (TC) as being the equivalent of the Russian S Class 2–6–2. It is not known whether these locomotives were converted to the broad gauge but, if so, a second conversion took place later, since they are stated to have been handed over to Eastern Germany.

The other types acquired and used in Russia included five classes of tank engine (Reichsbahn series 86, 91, 92, 93 and 94) dealt with in chapter 8. For the rest, the examples of the 38 Class 4–6–0, the 58 Class 2–10–0 and 55 Class 0–8–0 appear to have kept the whole of their German number; thus Reichsbahn 55·4399 has become U.S.S.R. 55·4399, either because there is no exact equivalent among the standard Russian locomotive classes or, more probably in this case, because the number of locomotives concerned is too small to justify the creation of a special class designation.

The other class concerned is the Reichsbahn 57 Class 0–10–0, of which the Soviet railways appear to have a fair number; several have been noted at work in Latvia. In this case the equivalent Russian class was considered to be the Shch (Щ) Class 2–8–0, with the result that the German locomotives are now known by the barely pronounceable designation ТЩ. An approximate rendering is Tshch, but this sounds like a person trying to stifle a sneeze.

Class TM (RUSSIAN TM)

Although Hungary took part in the war on the German side it does not seem that the Russian railways made use of captured Hungarian locomotives. Instead, that country was obliged to supply the U.S.S.R. with new locomotives, both of Hungarian and Russian design, built as reparations. The Russian type 0–10–0 locomotives have been dealt with in chapter 4, but the Hungarian design chosen was the 424 Class 4–8–0 of the Hungarian State Railways (M.A.V.). The equivalent Russian class to which they were assimilated was the Class M 4–8–0, and the Hungarian locomotives are therefore known as Class TM.

These machines were built by the Mavag Works in Budapest, from 1946 onwards, and differed from the standard version only in respect of their gauge and in being fitted with the usual Soviet automatic couplings. The quantity supplied is not known for certain but is probably about eighty or one hundred locomotives, numbered in a continuous series from TM1 upwards. About a dozen have been noted by travellers, mostly in and around the former Polish town of Lvov. It seems probable that this class was chosen only for the sake of quick delivery, until production could be turned over to the Russian class 0–10–0.

Chapter 7

POST-WAR CLASSES

The construction of main-line steam locomotives in the Soviet
Union since 1945 offers a parallel with that in Britain, for modern
steam locomotives were built in considerable quantities and the
final decisions, in both countries, to change to other forms of
motive power were not taken until 1955. Both countries offer
examples of construction to pre-war designs, to new standard
designs and to prototype designs for further building programmes
which were never carried out. At the beginning of the period the
fuel position in both countries was in some ways similar, neither
having large supplies of cheap hydro-electric power, and the case
for electrification was less strong than in countries thus supplied
but lacking their own large-scale coal reserves. Only when the
second Soviet post-war Five Year Plan brought vastly improved
fuel-oil supplies and large new hydro-electric stations did the basic
position change, and with it the railway motive power policy.

This chapter is concerned with the new designs evolved, but
we may first repeat briefly our previous references to the post-war
period. We have seen how, in 1945, the Russian railways obtained large numbers of existing locomotives as reparations from
Germany and Roumania, with some new construction in Hungary,
and now many hundreds of 0–10–0s were produced to what was
basically a pre-war Russian design in Hungary, Poland, Czechoslovakia and Roumania. In Russia itself there was also further
construction to pre-war designs, and we have seen how the post-
war examples of the Class SO 2–10–0 greatly outnumbered the
pre-war and wartime examples. From about 1945 to 1951,
Russian locomotive building works turned out about four hundred

2–6–2s to the pre-war Class Su design, and about two thousand six hundred Class SO 2–10–0s, all of which have been accounted for in previous chapters. But these locomotives of pre-war types are outnumbered by the locomotives built to completely new designs, whose total is thought to be somewhere between five thousand three hundred and five thousand six hundred.

Class L (RUSSIAN Л) *pl. 54, 55, 71*

The most urgent motive power need towards the end of the war was for a relatively powerful freight locomotive able to work over hastily-restored lines in the reoccupied territories, and capable of higher performance than the small-wheeled freight locomotives of Classes Er and SO. Because of this temporary downgrading of many lines in Western Russia, full use could not be made of the stock of heavy locomotives and some lines, which formerly permitted a 21-ton axle load, could now only accept 18 tons until the temporary bridges had been replaced by permanent structures.

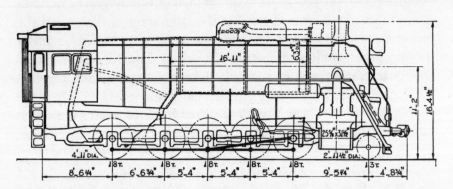

Class L

Faced with this problem of maximum output with minimum axle load, the Kolomna locomotive works evolved an excellent new lightweight 2–10–0 design, the first of which left the works on 5 October 1945. Comparative trials were held between the first two locomotives and an Alco-built 2–10–0 of 1944 on a section of the Moscow–Ryazan railway, at which (no doubt to the satisfaction of those concerned with propaganda) the Russian locomotive was found capable of a higher drawbar horsepower than the American machine. Since, however, the latter was basically a 1915 war-time design, with only minor modern refinements, this result should not have surprised anyone.

The new design was given the class letter P (Π) for *Pobyeda* ('Victory'), and the first fifty or sixty locomotives were numbered upwards from P·0001. In 1947 the class letter was altered to L (Л) after its chief designer, L. C. Lebedyanski. To make way for this renaming, the 'Pacifics' of the former Class L were re-classified Lp (see page 41). The letter P also occurs in a later series of designs, and was already in use on some tank engines, but as part of a different numbering system. A new feature on the L Class was the Boxpok type of driving wheel centre, which hence-forward became standard.

By every account, the Class L 2–10–0 has been an outstandingly successful design. Produced originally to meet a specific situation, it was later adopted as the standard post-war goods locomotive for main-line work, in place of a resumption of the pre-war 'big engine' programme. Details of the quantity produced by each builder are unknown, but it appears that the Briansk Works began a separate series at L.4001 in 1949 and built about twelve hundred while Kolomna and other works gradually filled in the lower numbers. Numbers have been observed in almost all ranges from 0001 to 5157, except for the 2500–2900 range, but there is little doubt that these also exist and that the total for the class is about five thousand two hundred machines, built over a period of some ten years.

DIMENSIONS
Cylinders 25$\frac{9}{16}$ × 31$\frac{1}{2}$ in. *Coupled wheels* 4 ft 11 in. dia. *Boiler pressure* 199 p.s.i. *Grate area* 64$\frac{1}{2}$ ft². *Weight full (engine only)* 103·8 tons. *Max. axle load* 18·2 tons.

More Big Engines

Despite this concentration on locomotives with an 18-ton axle load, the Soviet railways were very loth to discard their ideal of a 23-ton standard for trunk lines and, in 1944, a commission was set up to report on the advantages of a possible 23-ton axle load and the types of motive power and performance that it would make possible. It appears that they recommended the building of some prototype locomotives in order to obtain complete data, and in 1946 three locomotive works (Voroshilovgrad, Ulan-Ude and Kolomna) were asked to produce a design for a freight locomotive with an adhesive weight of 122–115 tons, and to build one locomotive of each design.

The three prototype locomotives were completed in 1948 and 1949 and submitted to intensive trials on one of the few lines already laid with heavy rail: from Osnova (the freight yards just south of Kharkov) to Krasny Liman in the Donets region. The Voroshilovgrad and Ulan-Ude machines were both of the 2–10–4 wheel arrangement, and were numbered respectively OR23·01 and 23·001, the 23 denoting the axle-load and OR the official title of the builders ('October Revolution Locomotive Works, Voroshilovgrad'). OR23·01 was an experimental design (see p. 95–6) but 23·001 resembles an enlargement of the FD Class.

The third locomotive, built at Kolomna, also had an adhesive weight of about 115 tons (actually, 117·5), but this was spread over six axles instead of five, the locomotive being a 2–6/6–2 Mallet simple, with an axle load of only 20 tons. It was slightly less powerful than the two 2–10–4s, but was presumably intended to represent the maximum performance obtainable for the lighter axle load. This locomotive was numbered P34·0001 (*pl. 73*), the P34 being its Kolomna Works 'project number'; the L Class 2–10–0 was Kolomna project 32 and we shall also meet projects 36 and 38.

The later history of the 2–6/6–2 is not known to the authors, although the two 2–10–4s were still shedded at Krasny Liman in 1954 and ended their days there. Another prototype at Krasny Liman was a 21-ton axle load 2–10–2 produced by Voroshilovgrad in 1954 and presumably intended as the forerunner of a new class for use on lines already open to the FD Class locomotives, but so far as is known, only two were built. These were numbered OR21·01 and OR21·02.

Class LV (RUSSIAN ЛВ) *pl. 56*

The decision not to build heavier locomotives can perhaps be considered as an indirect tribute to the designers of the L Class 2–10–0, the excellent performance of which greatly reduced the potential advantages of the larger machines envisaged. A rather more flexible edition of the L Class was required, with greater facility for running tender first and a larger reserve of boiler power. The 2–10–2 type was therefore adopted and, with a pony truck at each end, provision for altering the adhesive weight from 91 to 96 tons was incorporated. The axle load could thus be varied from 18·2 to 19·2 tons. At the same time the grate area was increased and a feed water heater added.

The prototype, numbered OR18·01, was produced by the Voroshilovgrad Works in 1952. This locomotive was later renumbered LV18·001 (LV denoting the Voroshilovgrad version of the L Class), and a further prototype was built and numbered LV18·002. Series production of the LV 2–10–2 began in 1954 and continued for some two years. Since the 'axle load' numbering system was less appropriate to the design with variable loading, the 18 was dropped from the title and the production locomotives were numbered upwards from LV0003. A maximum efficiency of 9·27 per cent has been claimed for these engines.

At the time when steam locomotive production ceased at the Lugansk (former Voroshilovgrad) works in 1956, the highest numbered example produced was LV.522, which was thus the last main-line freight locomotive built in Russia. When first delivered, these locomotives were allocated to the Chernorechenskaya-Krasnoyarsk-Zima section of the Trans-Siberian route and to the Magnitogorsk–Kartaly–Tobol line, both of which have since been electrified. They were then concentrated on the recently constructed thousand-mile Pechora railway to the Arctic centre of Vorkuta and remained in charge until dieselisation. It is probable that some are still there, on the less important duties.

Had it not been for the cessation of steam locomotive building in Russia after 1956, the LV 2–10–2 would probably have multiplied to a total of more than a thousand. However, the work involved has been put to good use, for many of the LV features have reappeared in a somewhat similar 2–10–2 class standard-gauge locomotive now in production in China. Since the first of these only appeared in 1957 it is a possibility that the drawings, patterns and machines for the LV were sold to the Chinese People's Republic when production ceased in the U.S.S.R.

As for the L Class, but with grate area increased to 69½ ft² and the weight full (engine only) to 121½ tons.

Class P.36 (RUSSIAN П.36) *pl. 57–59*

Throughout the Soviet period passenger traffic on the Russian railways has taken second place to freight; when the railways were unable to meet the demands thrust upon them by the rapid industrialisation it was the passenger services which were sacrificed, and many references in literature bear witness to the utter inadequacy of the long-distance passenger services and the consequent 'rationing', by permit or otherwise, of long-distance travel. This state of affairs persisted until quite recently, and until about 1954 the long-distance passenger services were inferior both in speed and quantity even to those of 1939–40, which themselves were barely sufficient to meet demands. Since 1955, however, there has been a large increase in passenger train mileage, and a study of the Russian time-tables shows roughly twice as many long-distance passenger trains today as were available in 1953, despite the very rapid development of Soviet internal air traffic.

This indifference to passenger traffic in the 1946–53 period was reflected in locomotive production, no further IS or other large passenger locomotives being built. Production was limited to a few hundred S Class 2–6–2s, as mentioned in a previous chapter, though the position was also eased during the period by some new suburban electrification, which released steam locomotives for use elsewhere. Neither were any passenger locomotives imported from abroad, except for one solitary 4–8–2 of the Czechoslovak State Railways Class 476·0, built in 1951 and presented to the Soviet Union as a token of friendship. This locomotive is named 'Друг' (*Drug* or 'Friend'), and does not appear to carry any other designation.

We have seen how, in 1930–31, trials with various new freight locomotives were followed by a decision on main-line axle load, which in turn was followed by a new standard freight locomotive class and then a passenger class. This pattern was followed again in 1947–50 and, after the decision not to adopt the 23-ton axle load, the Kolomna Works was given the task of building a prototype passenger locomotive with a drawbar horsepower of 2,500 and an axle load of 18 tons. The 'project number' allotted to it was 36, and when the locomotive appeared in March 1950 it was given the number P36·0001.

The new machine was a 4–8–4, the first of this wheel arrangement to appear on the Soviet railways. It was two tons heavier than the IS 2–8–4, but the additional carrying axle gave an axle-loading of 18 tons instead of 20, with a corresponding reduction in the total adhesive weight. Apart from the greater route-availability, its chief advantages over the IS 2–8–4 were in fuel economy and higher speed. It was the first Russian locomotive to be equipped with roller bearings throughout.

In 1953, after the restrictions on passenger traffic had been somewhat relaxed, it was decided to start production of these locomotives and the first, P36·0002, appeared in 1954. The 'project number' system of numbering was retained, perhaps because the death of Stalin was followed by a reversal of the practice of naming institutions of every sort after political personalities; had it not been for this, the new 4–8–4 would probably have been given another title. Two hundred and fifty locomotives of this class were built between 1954 and 1956, all at Kolomna, and the highest-numbered example P36.0251 (Kolomna Works No. 10420 of 1956) was the last main line steam locomotive built for the Soviet Railways.

The P36 Class (or the 'Type 2–4–2', as it is often known in Russian technical literature) is Russia's equivalent of our own Britannia-class 'Pacifics', in that it represents a versatile, medium-weight passenger design with many modern features and of quite pleasing appearance, which as the result of subsequent events has become the final culmination of the main-line passenger steam locomotive. The Russian railways are very proud of these machines, as well they may be, and concentrated them deliberately on the lines most frequently used by visitors to Russia, such as Moscow–Leningrad and Moscow–Minsk–Brest (Polish frontier).

Later, apart from a few at Lvov, they were transferred to the Trans-Siberian Railway and were working in 1970 between Ussuri, Khabarovsk, Skovorodino and Petrovsky Zavod. A few of the class are in the special blue livery, but most are in the passenger livery of light green with bright red wheel-centres and white wheel-rims, combining to give an impression not easily effaced. One of the authors has described elsewhere his excitement on first seeing one of these locomotives at Leningrad in 1957 and an attempt to capture the effect of these machines is made in the coloured frontispiece, based on first-hand observation during a visit to the U.S.S.R. in 1959. The medallion on the smokebox is of Lenin and Stalin, and the plate on the casing near the chimney is that of the builder (Kolomna Locomotive Works, 1955). It is strange that these fine locomotives have received scarcely any attention in the transport press of Western countries.

DIMENSIONS

Cylinders 22⅝ × 31½ in. *Coupled wheels* 6 ft 0¾ in. dia. *Boiler pressure* 213 p.s.i. *Grate area* 72·6 ft². *Weight full* (*engine only*) 135 tons. *Max. axle load* 18 tons.

Class P.38 (RUSSIAN П.38)

The decision to build large numbers of the lighter freight locomotives, instead of heavier types, has resulted in a considerable amount of double-heading on freight trains, and the visitor will sometimes be rewarded by the sight of a pair of Class L 2–10–0s heading a 3,500-ton freight train. The Russian railways are lavish in their use of manpower, so that double-heading is probably less unfavourably regarded than in other parts of the world, but ways have nevertheless been sought to reduce the practice by producing a locomotive capable of handling such trains unaided. Such a locomotive would require an adhesive weight of 160 tons, and since the maximum permissible axle-loading was 20 tons, an articulated locomotive with eight driving axles was indicated.

Working on this data the Kolomna Works, in December 1954 and January 1955, produced two large 2–8–8–4 Mallet locomotives, P38.0001 and P38.0002. The total weight of each locomotive in working order was 214·9 tons, with an adhesive weight of 164 tons, and the first locomotive proved itself capable on test of hauling a 3,500-ton train at 15 m.p.h. on a gradient of 1 in 110. With an overall length of 125½ ft, the impressive machines were the largest built in Russia. They were allocated to the Krasno-yarsk region, in Siberia, and were also tried between Baikal and Ulan-Ude. They are since stated to have proved too costly to maintain and to be unsuitable for very cold weather. Since the

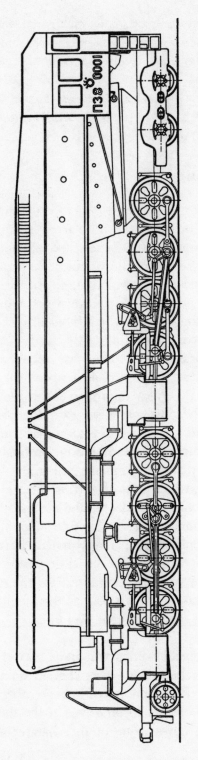

2-8/84 P38 0001

Drawing by A. E. Durrant

The largest steam locomotive built in Russia

line for which they were built was soon electrified, they were then transferred to the lines around Novokuznetsk, but were withdrawn from service after a relatively short life.

DIMENSIONS

Cylinders (4) $22\frac{5}{8} \times 31\frac{1}{2}$ in. *Coupled wheels* 4 ft 11 in. dia. *Boiler pressure* 213 p.s.i. *Grate area* 115 ft². *Weight full (engine only)* 214·9 tons. *Max. axle load* 20 tons.

The Change of Policy

In Britain, the decision, taken in 1955, to do away with steam traction, heralded an orderly transition from steam locomotive production to diesel and electric types, and existing orders for steam locomotives were allowed to stand; the last new steam locomotive did not appear until March 1960. In the U.S.S.R. the change was far more sudden, and within twelve months of the February 1956 party congress at which the decision was taken to stop building steam locomotives, all such activity had ceased.

The authors have not been able to find any full, official statement by the Soviet authorities giving their reasons for the change, though it is clear that the great improvement in the fuel position by the end of the second post-war Five Year Plan, especially the new oil-refining capacity, made a reappraisal necessary. Decisions on motive power in Russia clearly hinge on problems of a wider nature than mere railway requirements; they are linked to the so-called 'fuel balance', which aims at getting the most economical use of the various resources available, and almost all the newly-electrified lines, for instance, can be related to major power stations completed or under construction. The Russians have also stated that it is often cheaper to introduce diesel or electric power than to build more powerful steam locomotives, for the capital outlay on the new forms, although heavy, is less than would be needed to raise the standard of the permanent way to carry heavier steam power.

Clearly, all these considerations will have played a part. The first announcement of the change was contained in the figures for the third Five Year Plan, announced in September 1956, which showed only diesel and electric locomotives in the future building programme. Later the news value of the change of policy was recognised, and a typical comment is the following taken from *Soviet Weekly* for 11 December 1958: 'It really is goodbye to steam on Soviet Railways. Already all production of steam loco-motives has been ended for more than two years. In a few years' time steam trains will be found in the U.S.S.R. only in museums.'

The last new steam locomotive appeared towards the end of 1956 but it is apparent that opinion on this issue was far from unanimous. The sudden reversal of policy seems in fact to be closely linked with the fate of Mr Lazar Kaganovitch, the former energetic Commissar of Transportation and Heavy Industry, who in a 1954 speech defended his policy in the following words: 'I am for the steam locomotive and against those who imagine that we will not have any steam locomotives in the future; this machine is sturdy, stubborn and won't give up.' Less than three years later, all was changed, and Mr Kaganovitch was in disgrace, one of the charges against him being that he 'stubbornly insisted on developing steam traction, although it was well known that steam traction is uneconomic and outmoded'. In years to come his name will probably be honoured by steam traction enthusiasts, for his obduracy gave the world some most interesting steam locomotives. Within a few months of his removal from office main-line steam locomotive construction in the Soviet Union had ceased, probably for ever.

Chapter 8

TANK LOCOMOTIVES

The Russian Railways do not make a great deal of use of tank engines and it is possible to travel quite extensively in the U.S.S.R. without seeing a single example. Nevertheless, several classes do exist, but it is perhaps understandable that less is known about them than about the tender engine classes. Tank locomotives in Russia appear to be regarded as suitable only for shunting duties, especially in factory yards or docks, or as shed pilots.

The majority of Russian tank locomotives have always been owned not by the State Railways, but by industrial enterprises, whose combined railway systems in 1955 totalled no less than 48,500 miles of line. Some are ex-State Railway machines, others were supplied direct by various makers to their own designs; some are maintained by their owners, others by the State Railways, who also seem to operate a hire-service of industrial shunting locomotives from their own stock. The numbering of the locomotives is therefore of little help in estimating quantities.

Several types of 0–4–0 tank in use are probably all in industrial ownership, but the State Railway's stock included several types of 0–6–0 tank. Probably the oldest in 1959 were those of an 1899 class designated by the alphabetical symbol known to students of Russian grammar as the 'soft sign' (ь), a side tank design with an additional oil fuel or water-tank mounted on brackets above the boiler (*pl. 60*). Many other 0–6–0 tank designs were produced for industrial users between about 1901 and 1935, but in the latter year the Government seems to have decided that a greater degree of standardisation was called for, and drew up three designs which, it was thought, would meet all requirements. These were an 0–4–0 tank (Class 4P), a heavy 0–6–0 tank (Class 5P), and a light 0–6–0 tank (Class, 9P, *pl.* 61, 62).

In the event, only the 9P (9П) was produced in large numbers, beginning with a batch from the Kolomna Works in 1936. The total quantity produced is probably at least two thousand, but the numbering is a complete enigma, since examples have been seen carrying the numbers 9P37, 108, 257, 387, 9163, 10126, 10197, 13283, 16335, 17307, and 20466, which are probably their works numbers. Production continued at the Murom works until 1957, and the last of the class was also the last broad-gauge steam locomotive built in Russia.

DIMENSIONS of 9P

Cylinders 19 × 19 in. *Wheels* 3 ft 5 in. dia. *Boiler pressure* 185 p.s.i. *Grate area* 19·9 ft². *Weight full* 54 tons. *Max. axle load,* presumably 18 tons.

During the first Five-Year Plan (1928–32), three batches of 0–6–0 tank locomotives were imported into Russia, principally for use in the iron-ore fields of Kuznetsk and Magnitogorsk. These were given class letter T; two batches, each with sub-class letter g (for Germany) came from Henschel and Orenstein & Koppel, and the third, with sub-class letter a (for *Angliya* or 'England') were from Beyer Peacock, the order being placed to offset the development costs of the special Beyer-Garratt locomotive then being obtained from the same builders (*pl.* 63). The Beyer Peacock locomotives (the twenty 0–6–0Ts of 1931) were followed in 1933 by five 0–4–0Ts of the type shown in plate 64.

The tank locomotives taken over from the Baltic States and Poland have been mentioned in chapter 6, and the only other war-time acquisitions were some standard U.S. Army 0–6–0 tanks by Porter and Davenport, U.S.A. After the war, however, several types of tank engine were obtained as reparations from the Deutsche Reichsbahn and were mostly found in the Baltic States, States, perhaps on account of the customary use of tank loco-motives in those districts. The same method of renumbering was adopted with these locomotives as with the ex-German tender engines, namely a letter T for *Trofiya* followed by the letter of the Russian locomotive class to which they were considered equivalent.

Under this system the Reichsbahn 91 Class 2–6–0 tank was

considered the equal of the T Class 0–6–0 tank, and thus became Class TT. The 93 Class 2–8–2 tank was given the class letter Ъ (the 'hard sign' of the Cyrillic alphabet), which had been carried by a former class of 2–8–2 suburban tank engines (see p. 30) used around Moscow prior to electrification. The German engines thus became Class ТЪ. The Reichsbahn 92 Class 0–8–0 tank (Prussian T 13) was given the 'soft sign' designation of the Russian Tsarist 0–6–0 Tanks, although much more powerful than these, and thus became Class ТЬ, while two other German classes, the 94 Class 0–10–0 Tank and the heavy 86 Class 2–8–2 Tank, had no Russian equivalent and retained their German numbers (as in the case of the Class 55 and Class 56 tender engines). The only Class 86 locomotive seen in Russia now belongs to a steelworks, as do a number of ex-Austrian engines; where only a small number of a foreign class exist, the State Railways sometimes prefer to pass them on to industrial users in this way.

Chapter 9

NARROW GAUGE LOCOMOTIVES

Reference books on Russian railways make so little mention of the narrow gauge lines that the reader could be forgiven for thinking that none exist. However, there are many hundreds of miles of narrow gauge lines in the Soviet Union, which may be divided into the following main categories:

1. Common-carrier lines shown in the official Russian time-table as *Uzkaya Koleya* ('narrow gauge'), mostly pre-Revolutionary lines or networks now forming part of the State Railways.

2. Industrial, mineral, agricultural and forestry lines, often with passenger services but not worked by the State Railways or included in their time-table.

3. Children's Pioneer Railways.

The lines in the first category may be tabulated quite easily from the official time-table. There is the 2 ft 6 in (750 mm) gauge network in Estonia, totalling about 310 miles and serving a large area south of Tallinn, and a 220-mile network of the same gauge (with two isolated sections) in Lithuania. Latvia is less uniform, and the total of just over 620 miles of narrow gauge lines in that country is divided between the metre, 2 ft 6 in (750 mm) and 2 ft (600 mm) gauges, the second and third predominating. In Russia proper there is a 310-mile 750mm-gauge system south of Vinnitsa in the Ukraine, worked by the South Western Railway; three metre-gauge branches of the Moscow–Kursk–Donbass Railway at Tula and near Kursk; two metre-gauge branches of the Caucasian Railway west of Gori; and a 71-mile line running north out of Ryazan. In Siberia, the time-table shows a 60-mile line south-west of Omsk, probably of 2 ft 6 in (750 mm) gauge, and there is also the Emir of Bokhara's Railway from Kagan to Bokhara in Central Asia, described in Fitzroy Maclean's book *Eastern Approaches*. Finally there is the large 3 ft 6 in (1067 mm) gauge network in South Sakhalin (formerly the Japanese Karafuto Railway), taken over by the Russians in 1945.

Adding these together, we find that the State Railways have some 2,300 miles of narrow gauge line open to passenger traffic. The total locomotive stock is probably between six hundred and eight hundred, mostly steam. As on the broad gauge, the overwhelming majority are tender engines, including some post-war 0–8–0s and, in the Baltic States, some pre-war 0–10–0s, 2–8–2s, 2–6–2s and 2–6–0s often comparable in size and appearance to those found in Bosnia. The narrow gauge classes are designated by letters, but these do not seem to bear any relation to those of the broad gauge locomotives.

Tank locomotives of the 0–8–0 and 0–6–0 types were in fact supplied by a Belgian works when the Estonian lines were first built in 1894–98, but by 1930 only fifteen of these remained. The principal classes were Tsarist 0–8–0 tender engines by Kolomna and modern 2–8–0 tender engines by Krull of Tallinn.

The large Russian narrow gauge networks, such as those in Estonia and Lithuania, are less likely to succumb to road competition than are the narrow gauge lines of most countries, although a recent Russian pronouncement that road transport will in future be preferred for movements of less than 30 miles involving transshipment, may possibly bring about the demise of some of the short feeder lines. Apart from this, the main threat to steam on the narrow gauge lines comes from new bogie diesel locomotives now being built in Russia and Czechoslovakia for the 2 ft 6 in (750 mm) gauge lines in the Baltic States, on which steam has hitherto reigned supreme, little or no use being made of diesel railcars. Another threat is the conversion of lines to broad gauge, known examples being two lines north of Leningrad, the Dudinka–Norilsk Railway, and some in the Central Industrial District.

The Sakhalin railways are worked by standard Japanese 3 ft 6 in gauge steam locomotives, and when further locomotives were required a few years ago, the Soviet authorities very sensibly placed an order for further standard D51 class 2–8–2s in Japan.

Turning now from the State Railways' lines to those not under the control of the Ministry of Communications, it is much more difficult to be statistically or geographically precise; new industrial or forestry lines are constantly being discovered by chance reference in Soviet publications, while others such as the sugar-beet lines in the Ukraine are gradually being replaced by road transport. Newly-built narrow gauge networks include those linking the larger State Farms in northern Kazakhstan with their main line railheads (to handle the sudden bulk traffic at harvest time) and a system of forestry lines in the basin of the upper Kama. Mineral narrow gauge lines known to exist include Tetyukhe–Pristan (near Vladivostok), Sovyetskoye–Przhevalsk (near Alma-Ata), a line on North Sakhalin, another on the Mangyshlak peninsula (Caspian Sea), Bodaibo–Aprelsk (north of Irkutsk), and there must be dozens more. The 3 ft (914 mm) Kuishtin–Karabashskaya Railway, to which Henschel supplied some 0–6–0 tender engines in 1931, is also in this category. In 1955 there were said to be 48,500 miles of industrial railways in the Soviet Union, and although these were mostly broad gauge, it is likely that a good many narrow gauge lines were included in this total. As for the forestry lines, we have never seen any mileage figures for these.

In any other country the varied ownership and location of the narrow gauge lines would imply a wild diversity of gauges and motive power, but in the Soviet Union the centralised control of locomotive production and imports imposes a fair degree of standardisation. Thus, we know that the standard track used for these lines is 2 ft 6 in (750 mm) and that the standard motive power is a small-wheeled 0–8–0 tender engine (*pl. 66, 67*), those for forestry lines being fitted with spark-arresting chimneys. These locomotives are superheated and supplied in both wood-burning and coal-burning versions; they have a fully-enclosed cab and a dynamo to provide electric lighting. Most have been imported: five hundred and eighty-four were supplied by the Finnish builders Lokomo and Tampella in 1946–51 (together with a few 0–6–0s), and at least a thousand more have been added by Mavag (Budapest), Skoda (Pilsen) and by builders in Eastern Germany. In 1948 the Soviet Government wished to place an order for several hundred of these locomotives with the North British Locomotive Company (Glasgow), but our own Government were unwilling to provide the necessary export credit guarantee and the order was diverted to Hungary.

The industrial, mineral, agricultural and forestry lines are not subject to State Railways motive power policy, and will probably go on using steam traction for many years, especially where the waste from sawmills affords a ready supply of fuel. Narrow gauge forestry locomotives with spark-arresters were still being imported from Eastern Germany in 1958, nearly two years after main line steam locomotive production in Russia had ceased, and the total number of narrow gauge steam locomotives on these categories of line can hardly be less than two thousand. It may well be more.

So far as is known, the Russians did not seem to obtain narrow gauge locomotives from Germany as reparations or 'war-booty', probably because of gauge differences. They did however take over the locomotive stock of the 2 ft 6 in (750 mm) gauge lines round Königsberg in East Prussia, which are reported to have been abandoned and removed, and the retreating German army left behind some of its 750mm gauge *Heeresfeldbahn* machines.

The last category of narrow gauge line in Russia is the 'Pioneer Railway', a peculiarly Russian institution. These railways, of which there are now about forty-five, are located in the outskirts of most large cities and are administered by the local division of the State Railways as a cadetship scheme for schoolchildren, who work the line under the supervision of adult instructors. The lines are of 2 ft 6 in (750 mm) gauge and usually between 1¼ and 3½ miles in length. In the last decade, their coal burning steam locomotives have generally been replaced by diesel locomotives. The Pioneer Railways run only from early May to early September, and the stock is usually removed to the nearest main line railway workshops in Winter, for overhaul and storage.

Although the Pioneer Railways are miniature railways in most senses, their locomotives were generally of the standard 0–8–0 forestry type already described, though with rather more ornamentation. Every line seems free to use its own system of locomotive numbering and classification – class letters such as VL (Vladimir Lenin) are popular – and the pre-war Pioneer Railway at Minsk had an 0–8–0, contemporary with the high-speed 4–6–4s, and numbered '2–3–2' in the same way as an amusement-park railway in Britain might name its engine 'Royal Scot' (*pl. 68, 69*). This machine, built by an electrical works at Podolsk, was one of the first to be specially employed on a Pioneer Railway. The only earlier railway of this type, opened at Tbilisi in 1935, used what appear to be German locomotives of the *Feldbahn* type built by Orenstein and Koppel. The number of narrow gauge steam locomotives employed on Russian pioneer railways is thought to be between seventy-five and one hundred, and the total of narrow gauge steam locomotives in the Union can therefore be put approximately as somewhere between two thousand and two thousand eight hundred, of which about two-thirds are of post-war construction. Much however remains to be disclosed about them and a rich harvest awaits the first enthusiast who visits the little-known narrow gauge networks of the Ukraine and the Baltic States.

Chapter 10

CONDENSING AND EXPERIMENTAL LOCOMOTIVES

Condensing locomotives have been tried in various arid and water-less regions of the globe, but only in the U.S.S.R. and South Africa were full condensing locomotives in extensive regular use. In Russia the first application was on steam tram engines built at Kolomna in 1891. On these, part of the exhaust was passed through cooling elements, arranged in the form of a roof canopy, from which the condensate flowed back into the side tanks.

Such engines were only partial condensers. The first fully condensing equipment was installed on 0–10–0 Eg5224 by Henschel (Germany) in 1933, a new condensing tender being supplied, and the engine re-classified Egk (*pl. 65*). Two years later Kolomna began to construct condensing tenders and equipment for the SO Class 2–10–0s, the first two conversions, SO17·84 and 85, being completed in March 1936. The first classification SOk (COᵏ) was altered to SO19, the work was extended to other factories and various experiments were put in hand. In 1939, at the Voronesh repair shops, SO19·1245 had its reciprocating machinery temporarily replaced by turbines, SO19·961 was fitted up at Kolomna to burn pulverised coal and others were provided with steam air preheaters at the Rostov repair shops. The original intention was to build or equip two thousand locomotives with condensers, but the known numbers do not amount to this, being nearer one thousand two hundred, almost all of the SO Class. The use of condensing locomotives no doubt delayed the development of diesel power, remarkable in an oil-producing country. During the war the Germans ordered two hundred and forty 50UK Class with condensers for working in Russia, up to one hundred and seventy-seven being completed.

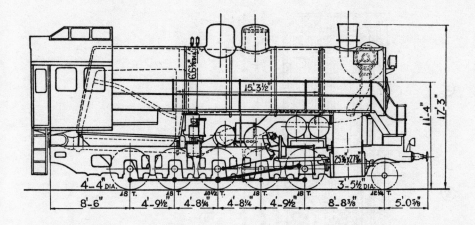

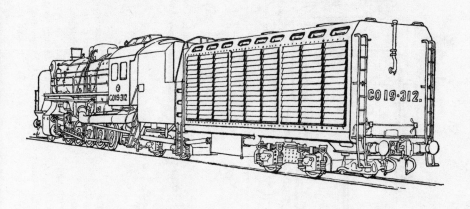

2–10–0 SO19.312

The working of a condensing locomotive is shown diagrammatically on p. 92. Instead of passing up the chimney the exhaust steam flows to the tender in a large pipe, which includes a grease separator, and also operates two turbine-driven fans. The first, of about 150 h.p., provides the draught for the boiler and the second, of about 500 h.p., drives the tender cooling fans. The exhaust finally passes through air-cooled elements on the tender sides to a hot well or into a main tank of about 5,000 gallons, provided to make up any wastage. As on a ship, blowing off steam is not

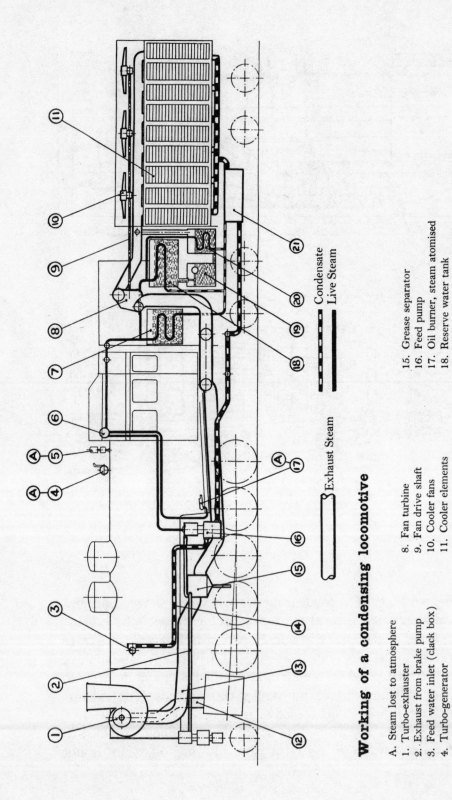

Working of a condensing locomotive

A. Steam lost to atmosphere
1. Turbo-exhauster
2. Exhaust from brake pump
3. Feed water inlet (clack box)
4. Turbo-generator
5. Safety valve
6. Steam fountain
7. Fuel oil (steam heated)

8. Fan turbine
9. Fan drive shaft
10. Cooler fans
11. Cooler elements
12. Exhaust from cylinder
13. Main exhaust duct
14. Feed line

15. Grease separator
16. Feed pump
17. Oil burner, steam atomised
18. Reserve water tank
19. Cistern for evaporator level
20. Evaporator
21. Hotwell and deaerator

━━━ Exhaust Steam

┄┄┄ Condensate

━━━ Live Steam

encouraged. The diagram shows equipment for an oil-burner, with additional details.

With the smokebox fan draught giving a higher superheat and the feed water temperature raised to 185–200°F, the condensing SOs were reckoned to save 10 per cent fuel over the non-condensers. There is also a considerable saving on boiler maintenance.

Apart from the SO Class a few more Em 0–10–0s were converted to condensers (Emk) at Kolomna in the 1930s and, in 1939, it was decided to alter ten of the larger FD 2–10–2s at Voroshilovgrad. However only two, FDk20·1546 and 2475 were completed, as the tender cooling surface was found quite inadequate for full power working and the smokebox fans wore out rapidly. For such engines as these, enormous tenders would be necessary and the project was dropped.

Condensing locomotives have been used in several waterless or bad-water regions mostly in the Urals (including the Ryazan–Ural line), Central Siberia (Omsk to Tomsk and around Karaganda), Central Asia (Ashkabad to Tashkent), Turkestan–Siberia and the North Caucasus. Their duties have been taken over since 1958 by diesel locomotives, but some have found further (non-condensing) work elsewhere.

Air pre-heating is another development on which the Russians have carried out many trials, as circumstances are exceptionally favourable. Not only does the very cold climate make its use economic but, on the practical side, the loading gauge allows ample space for unhampered ducting between boiler and frames. Air pre-heaters, by flue gases or by exhaust steam, showed a fuel saving of 5 to 6 per cent.

Experimental heaters were fitted to a number of Sum Class and some E Class engines, the earlier patterns from 1933 being heated by the flue gases with the usual blast pipe exhaust. Difficulties in keeping them free from blockage by cinders and ash led to trials with the alternative system of heating by exhaust steam. In this the exhaust is used partly to drive the smokebox draught fan and partly in air-heating elements situated around the firebox, the condensate being piped back to the tender. Such an arrangement was no doubt suggested by contemporary developments on condensing engines. Work on air pre-heaters was discontinued during the war (1941–6).

After the war air pre-heating was incorporated in a most interesting boiler designed by S. P. Syromnyatnikov who held that normal locomotive superheaters could not provide sufficiently high superheat. Chief features of this boiler are the short tubes, separate

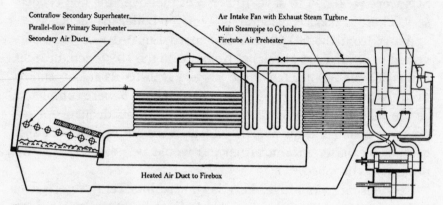

Syromnyatnikov Boiler

superheater chamber, integral air pre-heating and, externally, two separate chimneys. Designed originally for a proposed 2–10–4, a boiler of this type was fitted to 2–10–2 FD·3128m in 1952.

Another and earlier experiment involving two chimneys concerned 2–10–0 Yef127, rebuilt in 1935 with a separated superheater designed by I. V. Pirin. The boiler had a deep firebox with two large 25½ in diameter flues running along the lower sides of the barrel from the throat plate to a subsidiary superheater smokebox. The latter was placed in front of the normal smokebox and, being annular in form, gave access to the front tube plate. The elements were housed in the large external flues and the header in the base of the superheater smokebox, which also had an auxiliary blast pipe and chimney to produce the necessary gas flow. Such complete separation provided rather too high a superheat which caused various troubles such as cracked cylinders and eventually led to the scrapping of the engine in 1952.

In the 1930s and later many experiments were carried out on E Class 0–10–0s, including firebox siphons, circulators and water tube side walls, pulverised coal burning (on Eu701–83), feed water heaters and variant superheaters.

In the high pressure field a small 0–4–4T V5–01 (B5–01) was

built at Kolomna in 1937. Designed by Professor L. K. Ramzin, the boiler pressure was 1138 p.s.i. and the engine had geared transmission. In 1939 a much larger engine, a 4–8–2 with a pressure of 1422 p.s.i., was designed at Voroshilovgrad, but does not appear to have got beyond the drawing board. As regards valves, 2–6–0s Su 205–58 and 59 were fitted with the Lentz oscillating cam system in 1935 but, no marked improvement being found, the cylinders were later removed. In the following year Su204–71 was fitted with 'kinematic steam distribution', designed by N. I. Patlykh. This proved very satisfactory, particularly at higher speeds (62 to 78 m.p.h.), but unfortunately the authors have no further details. Piston valves of the Trofimov type have proved most satisfactory in Russia.

With the introduction of big engines having two outside cylinders the stresses imposed on the track became a serious factor. In America, developments tended toward division of the driving mechanism into two sets of lighter components. In Russia, with its lighter rails, a more complete solution was sought. By adopting opposed piston cylinders more or less complete balance on each side of the engine was aimed at, whilst direct action on the track was avoided by the interpolation of lay shafts in the framing. At the same time, the Still combined steam-diesel principle was incorporated, the engines being known as the Teploparovoz type. In these the outsides of the pistons were acted on by steam and the insides by internal combustion as diesels or by gas from a producer in the tender. Illustrations, however, would seem to indicate that uniflow steam cylinders were eventually fitted. These experimental arrangements are shown on p. 96 and will be self-explanatory to those interested. It will be noted that on the last arrangement, 2–10–4 OR23–01, the lay shafts and semi-diesel system have been eliminated for simplification.

This brief review will show that many steam locomotive experiments in Russia over the last thirty years have followed the general trend elsewhere. On the other hand, the most outstanding *differences* were the very extensive use of fully condensing engines, the development of air pre-heaters, separated superheaters and opposed-piston mechanisms.

opposed-piston mechanisms

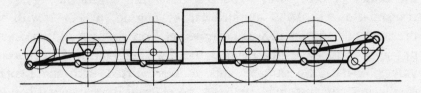

4-Cylinder 2–8–2 No. 8000 (1939)

8-Cylinder 2–10–2 No. TP1–1 *Stalinets* (1939)

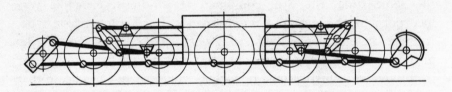

8-Cylinder 2–10–2 No. 8001 (1948)

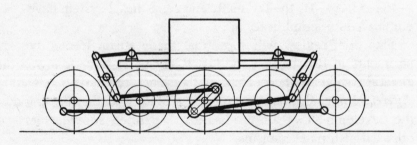

4-Cylinder 2–10–4 OR23–01 (1949)

Chapter 11

TAKING STOCK

Now that steam traction has passed its peak in the Soviet Union and the last new steam locomotive has entered service, it seems appropriate to end this account with a few words on the place which the steam locomotive has occupied in the Russian economy, both qualitatively and quantitatively. Its importance to the founding of the modern Soviet State can hardly be over emphasised, for the steam locomotive has until very recently been responsible for almost the whole of Russia's railway traffic, and this in turn represented almost 90 per cent of the whole inland traffic of the Soviet Union, freight and passenger.

Geographical and climatic factors have combined to give railways in Russia an importance far exceeding that which they enjoy in most other countries, for the absence of trunk highways, and the seasonal icing-up of navigable waterways, has made the railway the principal means of binding together this vast land area. Their vital strategic and economic importance also helps to explain the secrecy which for so long surrounded many aspects of their activities and even today leaves us to rely on estimation for certain of the facts and figures it would be interesting to have.

We have seen from chapter 7 how the building of new steam locomotives for main line service continued until 1956, and that several thousand new steam locomotives were built in the ten years before building ceased. Despite the electrification of selected lines and the use of new diesel locomotives, the steam locomotive twelve years ago still handled almost two-thirds of Russia's railway traffic; its share amounted to 97·4 per cent in 1940, 94·2 per cent in 1950 and 86 per cent in 1955. Then followed the change of policy and, by 1958, steam's share had declined to 74 per cent. A rapid decline followed to 57 per cent in 1960, 48 per cent in 1961, 38 per cent in 1962 and 15.5 per cent in 1965, at which date the final elimination of steam traction was expected to take place in 1970. This did not occur, and some steam locomotives were still in use in 1971; whether this was due to increasing traffic, deferred electrification, delays in laying heavier rail or other factors is not known. This has given a further lease of life to some excellent modern machines built since the war, but visitors in 1970 reported that for each steam locomotive still working, three or four could be seen lying derelict.

The study of work performed provides a most valuable guide to the total stock of Russian steam locomotives at any given period, especially where no official steam locomotive totals are available. The Russian railways publish figures for their output in terms of million freight-ton-kilometres, and the rapid industrialisation of the country has caused this figure to rise steadily since 1928 at a rate considerably in excess of that for most other lands; it is still rising fast today, in marked contrast to recent trends elsewhere. Since almost all this work was until recently performed by steam locomotives, it follows that the total stock of these has also been in constant progression, even allowing for the increased output of modern machines compared to the older ones which they replace.

From 1928 to 1937 the Soviet Union's stock of steam locomotives rose from seventeen thousand seven hundred to twenty-four thousand; ten thousand new locomotives were placed in service during this period and about three thousand withdrawn. The development of the railways was however outstripped by the simultaneous expansion of industry, and it was necessary to retain in service a great many old machines. By the end of 1940 the net total had probably risen by about a further three thousand three hundred, bringing the total stock to about twenty seven thousand five hundred at the time of the German invasion in 1941.

Although many locomotives were destroyed during the war, the Russian railways claimed to have successfully evacuated nearly all the more modern machines in the face of the German advance, and this is borne out by the fact that the Germans regauged the lines and built large numbers of locomotives for Russian service. At the end of the war the total locomotive stock had been increased through Lease-Lend machines, captured enemy property, reparations locomotives and locomotives acquired through the transfer of territory; after deducting war losses the 1946 total can hardly have been less than thirty thousand and may well have been more.

By 1950 the total railway traffic was almost exactly 50 per cent higher than in 1940, and the steam locomotive was still handling 94·2 per cent of it. This suggests that the total steam locomotive stock had risen to at least thirty-three thousand by that date. By 1955 the steam locomotive was handling 86 per cent of a total traffic figure 140 per cent higher than that for 1940, and even if we make the most generous allowance for increased operating efficiency and the greater output of modern locomotives, the total stock could hardly have been less than thirty-six thousand.

From 1955 to 1957 the total steam locomotive stock probably remained almost stationary, the new machines placed in service (six hundred and fifty-four in 1955, four hundred and ninety in 1956) being matched by roughly the same number of older locomotives withdrawn. Since the new engines were superior in output to those which they replaced, the total amount of work performed by steam locomotives continued to rise, and appears to have reached its all-time maximum in 1957. By 1958 the tide had turned, and the overall picture will be seen clearly from the following graph kindly prepared for us by Professor R. E. H. Mellor of Aberdeen University.

The zenith of steam traction in 1957 coincided very nearly with the placing in service of the last new steam locomotive and is the most appropriate point at which to assess Russia's locomotive stock. The 'standard date' which we have taken is 1 January 1958, and in the following table we shall set down the estimated total of each steam locomotive class at that date, and see how closely the result corresponds with the estimated total mentioned earlier of thirty-six thousand machines. Since that date the figure has declined by probably about four-fifths, but an exact assessment is rendered difficult by the fact that the majority of those surviving are used for shunting and transfer duties not readily apparent from the ton/km figures. It appears, however, that at the end of 1970, steam locomotives were still handling 3.5 per cent of traffic,

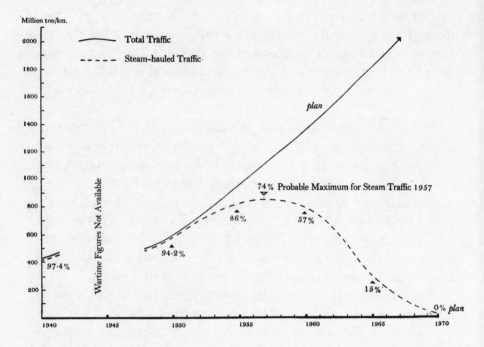

Total Russian railway traffic, showing proportion hauled by steam. The plan to eliminate steam traction by 1970 was not fulfilled and steam locomotives still handled 35% of traffic at that date.

against 48.8 per cent electric and 47.7 per cent diesel.

The following tables include only those classes numbering twenty or more locomotives, and where official figures are not available for the total number produced, an estimate has been taken from the number-ranges of those observed in service. The result is therefore subject to a possible error of up to about 10 per cent, and we shall be glad to hear from any readers who can correct or confirm the figures given, either from official sources or from actual observation. A further source of error is the uncertainty of the numbers of locomotives permanently lost through war-damage, for the very large figures quoted after the war evidently include many machines that were later repaired and returned to service. However, it is reasonable to hope that some of our errors may cancel out and that when official figures are released they will approximate to those we have estimated.

To this total we must add a figure for the other classes of steam locomotive known to exist: the various ex-Polish engines, those acquired from Roumania and the Baltic States, German classes

Estimated totals for each Standard Class as at 1 January 1958 (figures in brackets are conjectural)

RUSSIAN CLASS*	ENGLISH TRANSCRIPTION*	WHEEL ARRANGEMENT	YEARS BUILT	PROBABLE TOTAL BUILT	AUTHORS' ESTIMATE OF TOTAL IN STOCK AT 1 JAN. 1958
О	O	0–8–0	1891–1923	9,500	1,200
Щ, Щч	Shch	2–8–0	1907–1915	2,200	500
Н	N	2–6–0	1892–1913	1,000	20
Б	B	4–6–0	1908–1913	250	50
Ку	Ku	4–6–0	1911–1913	150	50
С	S	2–6–2	1910–1918	900	500
Э	E	0–10–0	1912–1925	(1,500)	1,200
Лп	Lp	4–6–2	1915–1926	66	—
Эг, Эш	Eg, Esh	0–10–0	1921–1923	1,200	1,100
Е	Ye	2–10–0	1915–1918	881	300
Су, Сум	Su, Sum	2–6–2	1926–1951	2,830	2,750
М	M	4–8–0	1927–1930	(80)	60
Эу, Эм, Эр	Eu, Em, Er	0–10–0	1926–1952?	9,500	9,200
ФД	FD	2–10–2	1931–1941	3,220	3,100
ИС	IS	2–8–4	1932–1941	650	600
СО	SO	2–10–0	1934–1954	5,000	4,920
Шᴬ	Sh, a	2–8–0	1943	200	190
Еᴬ	Ye, a	2–10–0	1944–1947	2,120	2,050
ТЭ	TE	2–10–0	1942–1945	—	1,500
ТЛ	TL	2–10–0	1942–1945	—	150
ТМ	TM	4–8–0	1946–1948	80	80
Л	L	2–10–0	1945–1954	5,200	5,200
ЛВ	LV	2–10–2	1952–1956	522	522
П36	P36	4–8–4	1950–1956	251	251

35,543

*including sub-classes where not listed separately

other than TE and TL and tank locomotives owned by the State Railways. The total of these is unlikely to be less than about eight hundred, and the resulting grand total is thus fairly closely in agreement with the estimate of thirty-six thousand quoted earlier as necessary to perform the work actually done.

The figures shown apply only to the broad gauge lines of the State Railways; were industrial and narrow gauge steam locomotives to be added, the resulting total would certainly exceed forty thousand. Even without these, however, the Soviet Railways for many years possessed the largest single fleet of steam locomotives in the world.

Appendix a

Some Railway Titles, Past and Present

Before the Revolution the railways, whether under State or private management, were run as separate systems. Afterwards the unified and expanding State Railway was reorganised into divisions, some of which more or less corresponded to the earlier railways although others of these older systems were dismembered. The purpose of these notes is to give the various titles under which some of the trunk lines have been known in different periods, the ' = ' sign being used, in each case, to separate the pre-Revolutionary from the post-1917 names. Lines that had little or no change of name have been omitted (e.g. Southern Railway = Southern Division; Northern Donetz Railway = Donetz Division), as have those where the break-up was very extensive (e.g. the Warsaw–Vienna Railway, or the Sysran–Viazma Railway, which was split up among four divisions). In Russia, however, these regional divisions are still usually referred to as 'Railways'. It should be noted, incidentally, that reference books prior to 1916 quote fairly large additional 3 ft 6 in and metre gauge mileages for some railways, but it would appear that most of these have been subsequently converted to 5 ft gauge.

Catherine or Ekaterinburg (*Yekaterina*) Railway =
    Stalin Division.
Far-Caucasian (*Vladikavkazkaya*) Railway =
    Ordzhonikidze Division.
Gryazi & Tsaritzin Railway = part of Stalingrad Division.
Moscow–Brest or Alexander Railway =
    Moscow–Byelorussian–Baltic Railway, now part of the Kalinin
    and Byelorussian (White Russian) Divisions.

Moscow–Nizhni Novgorod Railway = part of Gorki Division.

Moscow–Vindau–Rybinsk Railway = Kalinin Division.

Murmansk Railway = Kirov Division.

Ryazan–Ural Railway = (mainly) Kuibishev Division.

Samara–Zlatoust Railway =
  Ufa Division (and parts of the other Divisions).

St Petersburg (Petrograd, Leningrad)–Moscow,
or Nicholas Railway = October Division.

Urals Railway = Kaganovitch Division,
  later part of Sverdlovsk and South Urals Division.

Vologda–Archangel Railway = Northern Division.

NOTE: The Trans-Caucasian (*Zakavkazkaya*) Railway should not be confused with the Far-Caucasian (*Vladikavkazkaya*) Railway.

Appendix b

Russian Steam Locomotive Builders

NOTE † indicates the end of steam locomotive production.

1. ALEXANDROV *near St Petersburg (Leningrad)*.
   Built 225 locomotives between 1845–1870 and a further 106 intermittently up to 1893†. Also built rolling stock and other railway equipment.

2. LEIKHTENBERG Built 17 locomotives in 1851–1858 and, after reorganisation a further 22 in 1865–1874†.

3. KOLOMNA 72 *miles SE of Moscow*. Founded 1862. First locomotive 1869; 1000th 1887; 10,000th 1953. Built about 10,420 locomotives up to 1956†. First gas turbine locomotive G1–01, 1960. Also built coaches, bridges, river steamers and stationary engines.

4. MALTSEV Founded 1820. Built 373 locomotives in 1870–1881†.

5. VOTKINSK 200 *miles NE of Kazan*. Founded 1859. Built 124 locomotives in 1870–1883 and a further 441 in 1897–1917†.

6. NEVSKY *near Leningrad*. First locomotive 1870; 1000th 1882. Production was intermittent at various periods but built about 4500 locomotives up to 1941†. Locomotive works numbers begin at No. 1206. Subsequently built only small industrial engines. *Sometimes referred to as the Lenin Works*.

7. RAILWAY SHOPS Built locomotives between 1880 and 1917:
   a. ODESSA South Western Railway.
   b. ROSTOV Far-Caucasian Railway.
   c. TIFLIS Trans-Caucasian Railway.
   Rebuilding of locomotives was carried out at a number of Railway Shops.

8. BRIANSK 220 *miles SW of Moscow*. Founded 1873. First locomotive 1892; 1000th 1901. Built about 4850 locomotives up to 1941†.

9. PUTILOV *Leningrad*. Built 2577 locomotives between 1894 and 1930†. Also a shipyard. *Sometimes referred to as the Kirov Works.*

10. KHARKOV Founded 1895. First locomotive 1897; 1000th 1904. Built about 5000 locomotives up to 1941†.

11. SORMOVO *Nizhni Novgorod (Gorki)*. Founded 1849. First locomotive 1898; 1000th 1905. Built about 3850 locomotives up to 1952†.

12. LUGANSK 200 *miles ESE of Kharkov* (or October Revolution Locomotive Works VOROSHILOVGRAD). Founded 1896, in conjunction with the German Chemnitz Works. First locomotive 1900; 1000th 1906. Reorganised for building large locomotives 1931–1933. Built about 9500 locomotives up to 1956†.

12.a KRASNOYARSK *Central Siberia* War-time evacuation of Lugansk (Voroshilovgrad) (see No. 12). Built some freight locomotives between 1943 and 1945†. Subsequently engaged mainly on repair work.

13. NIKOLAYEV Shipyard. Built 44 locomotives in 1910–1912†.

14. ULAN-UDE *SE of Lake Baikal, Siberia*. First locomotive 1938. Probably built about 850 freight locomotives up to 1956.

15.   NOVOCHERKASSK 51 *miles NNE of Rostov-on-Don*. Principal electric locomotive builders, but turned out some steam 0–6–0T in 1941 and probably other industrial types.

16.   MUROM 170 *miles E of Moscow*. A repair works which started building small and industrial tank engines in 1946 and fireless steam locomotives in 1952. Built about 2,000 locomotives up to 1957 †. *Sometimes referred to as the Felix Dzherzhinsky works.*

Russian Locomotive Liveries

Drab colouring would hardly be in keeping with the Russian character, and old prints and models show plenty of colour on the railways in Tsarist times. Besides the more usual green and black engines there was a strong liking for red-brown liveries. Umber, red oxide, crimson and maroon were all used, some strikingly lined-out in broad white or broad black bands. The rolling stock was also gay. Pre-1914 travellers on the Russian railways say the 1st class coaches were blue, 2nd class yellow or brown and 3rd class green. Unique specialities of those days were the 'Mobile church' coach (with little turrets on the roof and painted in pastel shades with Orthodox Church symbols) and the blue 'Travelling clinic' and 'Travelling shop', whose wares supplied railway personnel and others in isolated regions.

Today there is still plenty of colour on the railways. Steam locomotives are black, bright green and (a few) light blue, often elaborately lined-out and usually beautifully kept. Most of them are black, lined-out in red, orange, red and white or red and yellow, but on small Tanks or old engines lining may be confined to the cab panel. Sometimes the tender beading is painted red, or the handrails white. In fact variations are endless, since such decoration seems to be left to the discretion of the crew or depot. Such variety certainly adds much to the Russian railway scene and helps to counteract the effect of the complete standardisation of designs. Smokebox doors have a dark red, white or golden star, those on the larger passenger-engines being dark red bordered with white and having a central bright medallion embossed with the heads of Lenin and Stalin. Smokebox rims or rivets are sometimes painted white and a few engines have brass boiler bands. Buffer beams are vermilion (sometimes lined-out) and buffers, black, with burnished or white painted heads. Tender panels or smoke deflectors may also carry emblems.

Wheels are generally vermilion with white rims and centres. Vermilion, crimson and black is used for the framing, and here again variations are legion. With the exception of the wheels and cylinders, the lower part of the engine may be entirely in one of these colours, but usually all three are used. In addition, the platform valence may be white (or cream), and one FD 2–10–2 (*pl. 42*) was seen with light blue smoke deflectors. Cow-catchers are often bordered with white.

Passenger engines of the P36 4–8–4, IS 2–8–4, S 2–6–2 and N 2–6–0 classes are painted bright green, with customary varieties of frame colouring, lining-out, etc. The P36s (see frontispiece) have a full-length crimson band bordered by two crimson lines, a decoration which has also been applied to some IS and S Class tenders. Embellishment is carried to extremes on Children's Pioneer Railways, where we have seen a locomotive with a large coloured portrait of Lenin mounted over the buffer beam (*pl. 68, 69*).

Lastly there are the striking light blue locomotives with silver bands and smokebox star, probably no more than a few dozen in all. In addition to the 4–6–4s, examples have been seen in all the main passenger classes – the IS Class shown at the 1937 Paris Exhibition was light blue – and in some cases the locomotives concerned were used to haul particular trains, such as the 'Red Arrow'. However, why the blue livery should be applied to a single 2–6–2 (*pl. 36*) at a country depot in Byelorussia is less easily explained, and it has been suggested that this may have been an honour accorded to the driver who had won some special award.

Russian locomotives are not individually named, although all the Joseph Stalin (IS) 2–8–4s carry his name in metal letters on the smokebox, and some of the Sergo Ordzhonikidze (SO) 2–10–0s have their sponsor's name in full on the buffer beam. The only individually named engines known to the authors are the Czech-built 4–8–2 *Drug* (see page 76), an experimental steam and diesel machine named *Stalinets* and one of the 4–6–4s which appeared on the twentieth anniversary of the October Revolution

(1937) and was christened 'XX October'. Political slogans, however, are sometimes painted on the tender sides or on part of an engine (*pl. 43, 72*).

Electric and diesel locomotive liveries have more basic varieties. Of the former, one of the most pleasing is the style of some large machines finished in royal blue, sparingly lined-out in vermilion with underframing varying from all black to all vermilion. In one trip from Leningrad to Moscow one of the authors noted three different electric and five diesel liveries, and an ensuing visit to the museum at the Riga Station in Moscow showed models all in further different styles!

Passenger coaches are green with broad white (or cream) bands, branch line stock being without the bands and showing considerable variation in the shades of green. Stock used on named expresses is usually red and yellow. Most goods stock is oxide red but cattle wagons are green, tankers black and refrigerator cars a pale cream yellow.

Transcription of the Cyrillic Alphabet

For easy reference the letters below have been arranged in more or less the order of the English alphabet rather than the customary Russian sequence. An effort has been made to give a different transcription for each Russian letter, to avoid duplication, the phonetic equivalents being approximate only.

RUSSIAN LETTER	TRANSCRIBED	PRONOUNCED	RUSSIAN LETTER	TRANSCRIBED	PRONOUNCED
А, а	A	b*ut*	О, о	O	s*o*rt
Б, б	B	*bee*	П, п	P	*p*ot
Ч, ч	Ch	*ch*urch	Р, р	R	*r*ace
Д, д	D	*deed*	С, с	S	*s*oap
Э, э	E	*egg*	Ш, ш	Sh	*sh*ore
Е, е	Ye	*y*es	Щ, щ	Shch	ca*sh ch*eque
Ё, ё	Yo	*yaw*n	Т, т	T	*t*in
Ф, ф	F	*f*ix	Ц, ц	Ts	si*ts*
Г, г	G	*g*o	У, у	U	f*u*ll
И, и	I	h*i*t	В, в	V	*v*eto
Й, й	I	ve*i*l	Ы, ы	Y	sh*e*rry
К, к	K	*k*ey	Я, я	Ya	*ya*rd
Х, х	Kh	lo*ch*	Ю, ю	Yu	*you*
Л, л	L	*l*oot	З, з	Z	*z*oo
М, м	M	*m*ore	Ж, ж	Zh	mea*s*ure
Н, н	N	*n*o			*table continued over*

	RUSSIAN LETTER	TRANSCRIBED	PRONOUNCED
Pronunciation signs	Ь, ь	—	(Soft sign)
	Ъ, ъ	—	(Hard sign)
Obsolete letters	Ѣ	Ĕ	*ye*s
	I, i	Ï	h*i*t
	V, v	Hy	*hy*pocrite
	Ѳ, ѳ	Ph	*ph*ial

NOTE: Readers of literature on Russian railways may sometimes be confused by the use of adjectival forms of place names, e.g. *Moskovsky*, *Moskovskaya*, *Moskovskoe*, etc. instead of *Moskva* (Moscow). Similarly, in Russian, reference would be made to 'the works at Kolomna' or 'the Kolomensky Works', but *not* to 'Kolomna Works'.

1. Locomotive shed

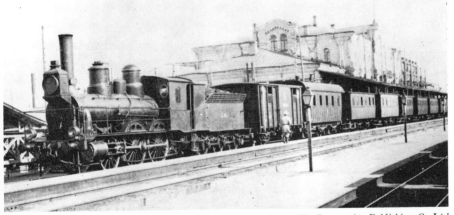

2. Local train

3. Trunk line express and a local train

THE RUSSIAN RAILWAY SCENE IN 1900

4. Ch Class 0–8–0s. One of the first standard classes in Russia

5. Gryaze and Tsaritsyn Rly. 0–4–2 Urquhart compound *drawing by J. C. Cosgrave*

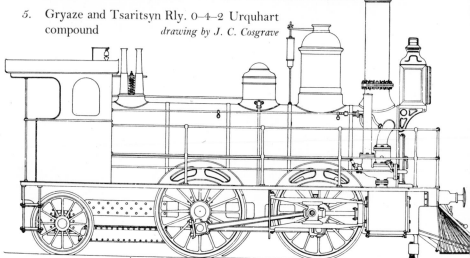

6. 0–8–0 Ov 4738

7.   0–8–0 Ok 7581 with piston valves   *photo J. O. Slezak*

8.   0–8–0 Ov 2241   *photo H. Fröhlich*

9.   0–8–0 Ov 5954

10. *below*   2–6–0 Class Nd with Joy valve gear

11. *below*   2–6–0 Class Ya—a contemporary of the N Class

12. *below*   2–6–0 Class Nu 9056 (old numbering) at Batum

13. 4–4–0 Tandem compound Class Pp

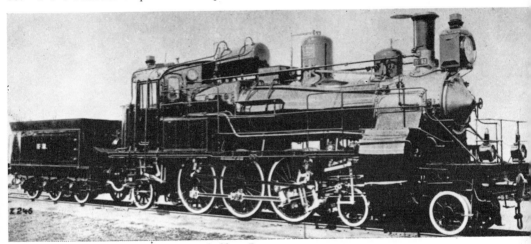

14. 4–6–2 4-cyl. compound semi-tank Class Pt

15. *below* 4–6–0 Class Ad with Joy valve gear

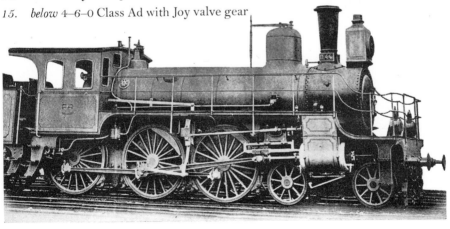

16. 0–6/6–0 Fairlie F 9803

17. Fairlies at Michailovo in 1919

18. 0–6/6–0 Mallet Class Ph

19. 4–6–0 Class B in Latvia in 1938   *photo L. R. van Rozenberg*

20. **4–6–0** Class Gp

21. 4–6–0 Class K with Savelyov valve gear

22.
2–8–0 Tandem
compound Class R

23.
2–8–0 Shch 347

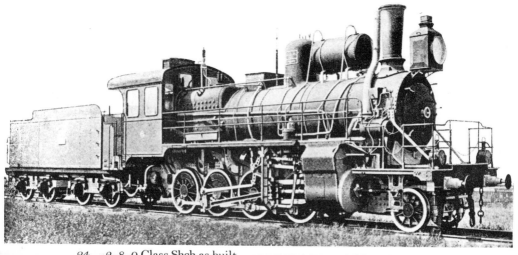

24.   2–8–0 Class Shch as built

25.
2–8–0 Shch 1573
photo J. O. Slezak

26.
Two Class Y 0–8–0s
on a heavy train

27.   Oil-burning 0–10–0 E 5465   *photo H. Fröhlich*

28. 0–10–0 Em 737–93

photo J. O. Slezak

29. 0–10–0
Er 789–22

30. 0–10–0
Em 735–07

31.　4–6–2 4-cylinder L 117 (later Lp)

32.　4–8–0 3-cylinder M 160–01

33.　*below*　2–6–2 S28—an early S class

photo H. Fröhlich

34. 2–6–2 Su 201–13

35. 2–6–2 Su
251–51 at Vainikkala
(Finland)
photo D. Trevor Rowe

36. 2–6–2 Su 100–49 in blue livery

photo H. Fröhlich

37.   2–10–0 Ye,l 1161 as delivered

38.   2–10–0 Class Ye   *photo R. G. Lewis (Railway Age)*

39.   2–8–0 Sh, a 194   *photo H. Fröhlich*

40. 4–8–2 + 2–8–4 Beyer-Garratt Ya–01 built at Manchester in 1932. At the time the lar

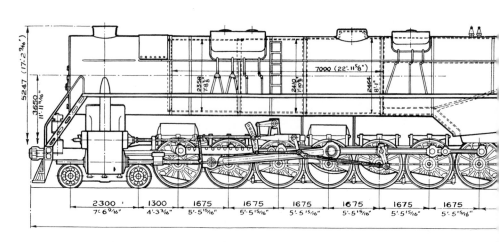

41. 4–14–4 AA20–1, built at Voroshilovgrad (Lugansk) in 1934. The largest non-articula

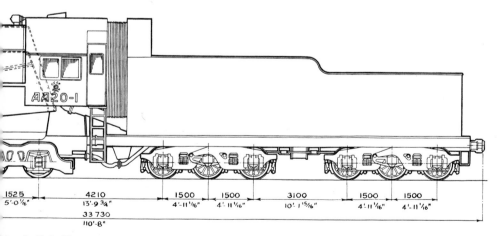

1525	4210	1500	1500	3100	1500	1500
5'-0 1/16"	13'-9 3/4"	4'-11 1/16"	4'-11 1/16"	10' 1 5/16"	4'-11 1/16"	4'-11 1/16"

33 730
110'-8"

42. 2–10–2
FD 20–2220
with light blue
smoke deflec-
tors and extra
decoration

43.   2–10–2 FD 20–2748 with both Boxpok and plain wheel centres   *photo H. Fröhlich*

44.   2–10–2 FD
20–1192
photo J. O. Slezak

45.　2–8–4 IS 20–84　　　　　　　　　*photo R. G. Lewis (Railway Age)*

46.　2–8–4 IS 20–578　　　　　　　　　*photo J. O. Slezak*

47.　4–6–4　2–3–2
No. 3 in blue livery
　　photo J. H. Price

48. 2–10–0 SO 18–3092

49. 2–10–0 SO17–2409   *photo J. O. Slezak*

50. 2–10–0 SO17–666   *photo H. Fröhlich*

51.   Ex-German 2–10–0 TE-5022   *photo H. Fröhlich*

52.   Ex-German 2–10–0 TE-1137.   *photo J. O. Slezak*

53.   Ex-Polish 2–10–0 Tu 23–312 at Lvov.   *photo J. O. Slezak*

54.　2–10–0 L–1084   *photo H. Fröhlich*

55.　2–10–0 L–0392

56.　*below*　2–10–2 LV–0026   *photo The Railway Gazette*

57.   4–8–4 P36.0006   *photo H. Fröhlich*

58.   Another view of P36.0006   *photo J. O. Slezak*

59.   *below*   4–8–4 P36.0115

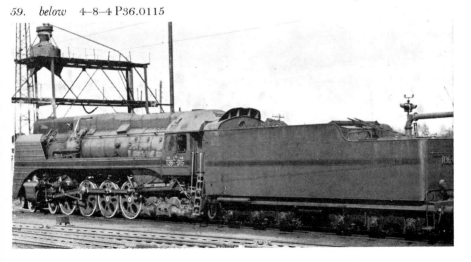

60. Old 0–6–0 T (soft sign) 9793   *photo J. O. Slezak*

61. 0–6–0 T 9P–10197   *photo J. O. Slezak*

62. 0–6–0 T 9P–108   *photo H. Fröhlich*

63. 0–6–0 T Class Ta　　　　　　　　　*photo Beyer, Peacock & Co Ltd*

64. Heavy 0–4–0 T for industrial service　　　*photo Beyer, Peacock & Co Ltd*

65. Condensing 0–10–0 Egk 5224 as rebuilt　　　*photo Henschel & Sohn*

66. Children's Pioneer Railway, Leningrad 750 mm. gauge forestry type 0–8–0

67. Children's Pioneer Railway, Leningrad 750 mm. gauge 0–8–0 built in Finland, 1947

68. Children's Pioneer Railway, Minsk 750 mm. gauge 0–8–0 built at Podolsk in 1936

Note portrait of Lenin and engine number of crack 4–6–4 class

69. Children's Railway, Park of Culture, Minsk

photo J.H. Price

70.
FD class 2–10–2
under conversion to
standard gauge at
Changchun Works,
China
photo The Railway Gazette

71.   Two L class oil-burning 2–10–0s on heavy freight train   *photo J. O. Slezak*

72.   Oil-burning 2–10–0 SO17–42 with O class 0–8–0 behind   *photo H. Fröhlich*
Note central couplers and slogan on tender for "World Peace"

73. 2–6/6–2 P34. 0001

photo J. O. Slezak Collection

74. 2–8/8–4 P38. 0001

The last main line steam locomotive type built in Russia

75.   2–6–2 Su 208–87 on local passenger train   *photo H. Fröhlich*

76.   Across the steppes behind a Su class 2–6–2

77.   4–8–4 P36. 0055 about to cross the Moscow-Volga canal

THE RAILWAY SCENE IN RUSSIA TODAY